How I met my Guardian Angel

LisA

remmber Friend will
Always be with you...
My best Friend

Robert

X X X

Praise for How I met my Guardian Angel

It's a long time since I was given an angel book that was so readable, so down to earth, and presented with such honesty and humility. Written retrospectively, having awakened to his true soul purpose and the divine gifts of healing and clear-sight; having experienced so many life affirming spiritual phenomena, as well as the ecstatic highs and soul wrenching lows of a troubled journey ... this book comes straight from the heart.

It expresses part of a young man's life story; full of the drama and self-indulgence of escapism, the emotional suffering, love and pain that is so often experienced by someone suppressing their spirituality and true life purpose, and takes us to an amazing and beautiful realization and outcome.

Robbie's wonderfully Irish, page turning story-telling style bravely reveals a deep vulnerability which actually moved me to tears at times, spontaneously laughing out loud at others.

My favourite part of the book, not surprisingly, were the angelic encounters with Robbie's guardian angel which for me brought tears of pure joy and connection. The sheer clarity, depth and beauty of these words of wisdom, given by Robbie's angels to share with other seekers on the road ahead, really are divinely inspired. There is no doubt that the angels words, through Robbie's reflection, will echo with a resonance that will make the hairs on your neck stand on end. As you read them, and they speak to your heart, they will call to your soul, and remind you ... that faith, hope and love are truly all that matters.

Chrissie Astell
Best Selling Spiritual Author, Teacher and Facilitator

This book is an absolutely fascinating read, Robbie holds your attention throughout every chapter as he entertains, inspires and shares his most intimate thoughts with you. It is jam-packed with comedy, tragedy, drama, out of this world experiences and peppered with words of wisdom.

How I Met My Guardian Angel is one of those books you will read all the way through and still want more.

I am really looking forward to the sequel.

Stevey McGeown
known as Ireland's Number One Results Coach

"How I Met My Guardian Angel is the poignant journey of a young man's struggle against substance, fear, angst, pain and dark depression. Starting in Ireland to his time in America where he met life- threatening, tragic and changing situations, the events eventually culminate in him meeting with his Guardian Angel and the start of his awakening.

Robbie H Andrew's offers the reader a no holds barred account of his true story laying bare his soul, at his darkest hour that the reader cannot be moved by the traumatic happenings. Told with humour and wit and utter amazement the author depicts his experience in a way that you feel you are there with him. The added dimension of musical interlude throughout the book really sets the mood and scene of the particular moment.

Whether the reader is spiritually minded or not I suggest that this uplifting read is charged with emotion that all can relate to at some point in their life that they won't be able to put it down. This story sends out the true message of HOPE"

Arlene McWilliam Green
Poet and Business Woman

HOW I MET MY GUARDIAN ANGEL

Robbie H. Andrews

Urlar Publications

Urlar Publications

Copyright © Robbie H. Andrews

Robbie H. Andrews asserts the right to be identified as the author of this work

ISBN 978-0-9573395-3-8

Typeset in Shannon by Compuscript Ltd., Co. Clare, Ireland
Printed and bound in Ireland by EPrint Ltd., Blanchardstown, Dublin 15

Cover by the Artist Ciaran Dunlevy, Drogheda, Co. Louth

A CIP catalogue record for this book is available from the British Library
www.urlarpublications.com
www.facebook.com/urlarpublications @UrlarPublications

In life, we spend most of our time waiting for the magic to happen. For me I have realised that I am the magic and all I have to do is believe.

I don't know how to do this book the justice it needs or have the best words to describe it but I guess if you could turn golden light and all that was complete bliss into a book, this would be it. This is 50 shades of heaven.

It is simple beauty at its best on every level.

Lorraine McMorrow

I dedicate this book to you, the reader. May the love of God always shine through you and bring you H.O.P.E

Acknowledgements

This is the part of the book where I get to give a heartfelt thank you to everyone who has helped me along my journey. There have been so many friends and family members, my beautiful Guardian Angel and Angels, Spirit Guides, God and the Universe all supporting me every step of the way, but first I must start with the people who are closest to my heart ...

I want to thank my beautiful partner and best friend, Michelle who has been my rock and has supported at every single moment. There is not enough words to say how much you have helped me and the patience you've shown. This book would not be where it is without your amazing editing skills. I am so grateful that Angels brought us together. I love you my sunshine girl.

Thanks to our little dog, Mia who has sat lovingly beside me whilst every single word was typed. Mia is such a great listener!

Thank you to Mother and Father God and the Universe for sending me my Guardian Angel and the sacred bond we share. There is one thing that I will never share because of our sacred contract, that is, my Guardian Angel's name.

Thanks to my Spirit Guides Danny and Tommy who have taught me many lessons of understanding and compassion. Also I would like to thank all the wonderful Angelic beings and my Spirit family.

Thanks to my mother, Jacinta and father, Heno, who I love dearly and have truly taught me many great lessons in this lifetime. Thanks to my brother Joe, my sister Vicky and little brother Jason for standing behind me even in times when you thought I was crazy! I never stopped feeling the love you have for me. Thank you. I love you all.

Thanks to my sister-in-law Sinead and brother-in-law Nick. Sinead I really appreciate your help earlier on in the book. I don't think I've met anyone that can type as fast as you!

A big thanks to all my nephews, Emmett, James, Cian, David, and nieces, Teegan and Sophie.

Thank you to my Grandfathers, the late Paddy Walsh and Harry Andrews who now share their time helping others in the Spirit realms. A special thanks to my Grandmothers Sarah Andrews and Nancy Walsh. I've been very lucky to have nearly all Grandparents living for the most part of my life. Nanna Walsh, you have been such an inspiration to me in this life. I have learned so much from your love and wisdom. I will be eternally grateful for every moment we have shared. I Love you.

A massive thank you goes to my uncle Brian and Aunt Tammy. You were the hand that reached out to pull me towards a light in a dark time of my life. You helped me see and feel the bridges I needed to cross to get me on the path to where I am now. Thanks to Neala McPhail for making that phone call and being a best friend forever. To my good friend Kerry Kennedy for your tremendous support. To my childhood friend Lee, thank you for being there. To my Aunt Ann Henry, thank you for being a best friend and the great conversations we have shared and will share. To my soul friends Roselind Trodden, Eddie Barrett and Deirbhla Clarke, thank you for that circle of friendship and all you have given me. Thank you to my Aunt Jackie Rice for introducing me to Bernie Doyle. Thank you to Bernie "Save it" Doyle for all the help you have given me and the push I needed to continue writing my story. Thank you to Sandra Poland Barry for the beautiful poem "The Sign" that you channeled from the angels and has a pride of place at the end of this book. Sandra, we will always be friends.

Thank you to Edmond and Goretti Carroll for introducing me to a most amazing publicist and friend Lorraine McMorrow, to the universe for bringing us together through the publishing company Urlar Publications.

To Ciaran Dunlevy for bringing that astounding talent to the cover of my book, thank you. Thanks to my very good friend Stephen "spoke" Gearthy, Lisa and your daughter Summer. I am so grateful for your support. To all the people who for one reason or another have been a part of my life I extend my heartfelt gratitude and love. To the following wonderful people that have so kindly reviewed my book: Arlene McWilliam Green, Dr. David Hamilton, Chrissie Astell and Stevey McGeown.

Contents

Preface

My Story

My name is Robbie Andrews, I'm 33 years young—I'm alive, I'm awake and I'm living in the knowing of my own truth.

From the day my Guardian Angel crossed over to meet me physically to bring me a very sacred message and give me the most special gift that would change my life forever, my life has been touched in so many ways I could never have imagined. As I finally share my journey with you from the depths of darkness to the greatest light of all, holding on to my truth hearing *'your time will come'*. I've waited patiently for many years listening to my Guardian Angel, waiting to hear these words *'The time is now'*.

Bringing our message from the Angels, it is one that is most needed on our planet right now!

As I share my story I ask *'What can I tell you that would help you?'* How can I share the knowledge I've learned to help you overcome the many obstacles in your path? Helping you feel you have a purpose in your life which will come.

This story begins in my early 20's; I will bring you back through some events in my life to give you an understanding of how and why I'm here. In the depths of my darkness I found a glimmer of light that would eventually bring me back to the place in my life that had meaning. *'Only through my darkness could I find my light'*. The hurt, the pain, the anger, and self-destructive patterns would finally get the chance to be healed. Underneath I had to work my way through the patterns of my past, present, and look into my future. The feeling of being so lonely, crying for help and for someone to understand how I felt. *Why had I so many questions but could not find the answers?* Finding them was the part of the journey I would have to partake in.

Why has God abandoned me?
Why is this world so unreal to me?

Who writes the rules we're living in?

Why did I feel God was something that existed outside of me?

Like there was a separation between God and me. It felt like we were two different things, separate entities. It was like the God I was taught about belonged in a book and this never felt right for me. I struggled to connect to these teachings. I found myself moving away from God, yet on the other hand, somewhere deep in my being, I longed to find out what I really felt within my soul. I asked myself: *does God really sit on a throne?* I remembered the words I had heard so many times in my life—that we are all children of God and the love God has for us has no bounds. Yet I couldn't connect to this God in a book or on a throne because somewhere within I felt disconnected and out of harmony. I felt like there had to be more to this life but then on the other hand, what if there isn't? I had this on-going battle -struggling to find validations in my life or some sort of truth.

In this world of emotions I felt no way of expressing what was going on the inside or externally. A feeling that I was being misled or misleading myself to find someone or something, a channel even, to blame my misunderstanding of who I was. *Why does this place have to be so hard?*

The Angels of HOPE and I will be taking every step with you; to help you find a meaning and a sense of belonging. There will be highs and lows, ups and downs, and some crucial points in my life that brought me to write my story with the help of my Angels. **"How I met my Guardian Angel"**.

I have so much to share and I hope that my story is one that will help you to open your eyes, your hearts and minds. The realisation is that we can all change and become so aware that there is no emotion we cannot conquer through wisdom and experience.

We have to walk in our own truth and self-belief, and not that of others.

Remembering who we are is more important. How can we open our eyes to our hearts and minds so we can become more aware of who we are within our hearts and souls? The Angels of HOPE say it is very important for us to see? But in these words we miss the essence of ourselves.

We may have mislaid our truth of who we really are and what we are capable of as souls having a human experience. Everyday modern life through different forms of media and communication, have portrayed what they want you to see and believe, but what if there is so much more when you start experiencing and seeing things differently for yourself?

The answers we seek may lie in our emotion, and to really see who you are, your divine self, your God spark illuminating to the world.

To do this, to find your answers, then it's important we understand our world and our emotions. This is a time on earth that we are urged to take down the barriers which have surrounded us for many life times, to break through the illusion and really see our true power. This is the essence of who we are and what lies within.

These words have a very powerful meaning, yet are still so misunderstood. **The light and the truth and the way, what do they mean I ask?** Seeing the words is important but more importantly is to feel them. Knowing your essence from where you came, the grace of source or God that is within you, from both Mother and Father. You are your own master. Can you accept this part of you? Can you handle your inner power and take back the control from other forces? Are we afraid of this? Are we afraid of being empowered and using it for pure goodness? For so long people have been disempowered so that others could control. Religions told you God was to be feared and outside of you, a separate being of power. But I know this is not true, for every soul has equal God within them, no one soul is more special than the other on this earth. Look within for God, not outside. Take back your God Power!

You are your creator—can you accept this too? You and you alone are the one who leads by your example. It is time to walk your way out of the veil of illusion and into the light that you are. My message to you is one of HOPE sent to me by my Guardian Angel. I will explain the meaning and how I have found my answers.

I will share this message with you as I tell my story. My story begins in my early 20's and I will take you from there on my whirlwind journey!

Life is not a project it's a reality, but in the midst of life you may find many projects and realities

1

Every Beginning Has a Story

I was living in a small town called Drogheda, Ireland. I was so lost
with no understanding of my purpose or what it meant to be living a
full life; I felt I was stuck on a conveyer-belt. During this period, I, like
many other young people, was living a life with very little meaning. I
was in a dream world, out of touch with myself, living life in a bubble,
thinking and feeling that I was invincible or bulletproof, that the world
owed me something. Yet somewhere deep inside I knew I wanted to
find my place in the world. This process meant I was going to take a
few knocks and bangs to open my eyes!

As a child I seemed to float under the radar of school, unnoticed.
I was a right-brain thinker so the left brain of logic education was
foreign to me. As I couldn't really connect with it I switched off from
it in a way. That then left me with a lack of communication and no one
to guide me or teach me in the way I needed. Writing English became
a problem for me but the adults seem to be OK with letting me drift
along and I sure was OK with that at the time. I can see this now but at
the time I had no clue what was happening.

My life mostly consisted of taking drugs. I was living a double
life—Happy on the outside but in so much pain on the inside trying to
understand the duality of this world. I was living a life that couldn't
have been further from my truth. I had no understanding or didn't
know who could help me. *What am I saying?* I didn't even think
I needed help! For me, I always felt like I slipped under the radar.
This all stemmed from my childhood. However, contradictory as it
may sound, somewhere in my being I was aware that something was
missing and my truth would look for me.

I was always very different. I felt this as a child right up to my teens.
How different my life was going to be would not be fully exposed until

my early 20's. During the time leading to this I felt like two different people, there was the kind child Robbie inside that wanted to be loved and not feel lost hurt or angry. What I portrayed to the world was a jack the lad, never in trouble, but finding myself in and around trouble, never really understanding why? I was hurting, and finding myself around people who were also hurting.

For me, taking drugs was most definitely a complete form of escapism. I had come through so many experiences up until this point. I started taking drugs from a young age, just like a lot of other young people around me; it seemed to be the way to go, always hiding from one aspect of my life, but to others I was the one who was leading the way. Drugs became my escape. When I look back now, I can see where God, the Angels, and my Spirit family were there to help me. They have truly never failed me throughout my journey, I just couldn't see this until the day I met my Guardian Angel. I will return to this later in the story.

My childhood was an explosive one with lots of different hurts and pains. I come from a family of two brothers and one sister. I am the second eldest with my older brother Joe, younger sister Vickie and the baby of the family, Jason. My parents were hard working. Henry, my dad, worked in a factory and drove a taxi. My mom, Jacinta worked in factory as a cleaner. She was a very proud house-mom. Growing up in my family wasn't an easy process and there always seemed to be some sort of hurt or pain for me. I never could understand why there was so much tension in my family home, and why as a family unit we were often in heated arguments? The answers for my childhood and the 'things' I experienced would not come to me until my Guardian Angel and Spirit family would enter back into my life. I had second sight as a child but at that time I had blocked this awareness from my life due to my experiences and it lead me to the opposite end of the scale, to scepticism. My childhood was such a blur to me and there was also the part of me hiding the hurt and pain from my experiences. I had been trying so hard for the most of my life to understand why I felt so disconnected from my parents and the love I felt inside of me was not what I was experiencing in my world. Love was not expressed in our family so it didn't have an outlet for me. I didn't hear the words "I love you". Finding the answers and the soul that is within would bring me on a journey I could never have foreseen.

When my Guardian Angel came to me, I was at a point in my life where I had lost all faith. I was feeling so damaged—this is when my Guardian Angel helped me to get my life back into a place of harmony—*only through my darkness could I find my light*. We as humans have so many different emotions that we feel and how we use these in our life can determine which path we take. We all know how the wind can blow on our face in one moment; the next thing you can't find a breath, feeling like you're suffocating, like your life is slipping away. Has anyone ever told you it's okay just to be you? Has anyone said the reason you don't understand is because I never understood so I couldn't explain to you? We have all felt many emotions through our misguided understanding of life, how the rights and wrongs of people's judgement's project on our journey. Some are positive but in my case most were not.

I am here to help all who encounter me in this lifetime. Helping them to really see their true light, their value, understanding that it's okay, it's time to take charge and to start to live your life in a way that has complete meaning. You will find the strength and courage to bring you through this day and the next. I know this because my angel told me this and helped me and this is the reason I can help others. It's not that I am wiser than you, it simply means I have been in darkness and emerged the other side into light.

Lean on me for I am standing tall today and my light will bring you through the perils of your darkness, only to let you see how bright you shine. Lights shine to guide the way, not to take the light away from others.

HOPE—it's in HOPE that we will find ourselves.

(Song—*I grieve* Peter Gabriel—from the movie "City of Angels")

In October 2000 my grandfather passed away after a battle with cancer. He was only properly diagnosed two weeks beforehand.

Towards the end of his life there was a great deal of pain. My mom's family was a large traditional Irish family of 9 boys and 5 girls. Watching my grandfather fade away so fast was so painful. I loved him so much. I didn't understand why the world could be so cruel to have him taken away in a great deal of pain and so quickly, this was unbearably painful for all our family.

In life we know people come and go all the time. It's only a reality when it happens to someone close to you. So when we see others losing their loved ones, we never quite get the full measure until death knocks on our door. Why does there have to be so much hurt?

I was breaking down inside, this was my first time experiencing great loss. Even though there had been other deaths in the family, this was my granddad, my friend, someone I loved so much. He was the one who had always seen through my walls. He knew all my tricks and could see my internal pain. My grandmother was a tower of strength and faith for us all. Watching her loose the love of her life tore me apart. I loved my grandmother unconditionally. I felt that he was gone forever as well as the bond we shared. I felt so alone at this point and my belief system was very little to none. These things offset my emotions. How was I to understand when I lived a life that was so out of balance? I am living in my family home and as a unit things were hard for us. I grew up in a place where the only emotion that we could properly express was anger. I couldn't understand this. What was the missing link in connecting me to my father, mother and siblings? Why did we fight when underneath we loved each other? Why did we hurt each other so much when we loved each other so much more? My world was so confused and for me wanting to run away was my escape. My answer to this at that time was taking drugs, drinking, seeing no value in myself. I grew up thinking and feeling we were the only family on the street who fought. If there was an argument in the house at night when I went to bed, I thought the world could hear it, so when I went out I thought people knew our business.

All these fears, seeing the world through the eyes of fear, in a place of fear, feeling trapped.

Somehow ending up believing that when you die, that's it, you're done.

Whoever came back from heaven and said it was real?

Why has life no meaning and who can answer my questions about life?

Why was I so hard on myself?

How could my life not be the perfect thing it was meant to be?

Why did I feel like a failure?

Why had I so much fear?

Why could I not feel loved? What's holding me back?

The list continued until the day God sent my Guardian Angel to intervene in my life. The only way God could intervene was when I gave God permission to help and a reason for God or the source of who we are to answer me. Don't we all ask these lists of questions at some point in our lives? For some of us, it's more real than others, this feeling or thinking that we are all separate to all things in the world and most of our teachings back this up. From children we are taught that God is separate, God will punish you if don't love him or he will send you to hell if you're a sinner. We are all asking the same questions and trust me, we are all receiving the same answers. It's time to help you to take down the veils of disillusion. There is a God, but God is so personal to you, only you will ever truly understand. God is unconditional love there to guide you every step of your way but you have to be always true to you. "To thy own self be true". The only one true meaning that is you, and you alone hold the truth. So it's time for you to look deep within and the answers you seek you will find.

I spent the following months after my granddad died just stuck in this emotional rut that I was in for most my young adult life. I was in a not so happy relationship. After Christmas of 2000 the relationship started to fall apart, it was ending. The feeling of being rejected was really tough, my inner child was taking a beating with all the different emotions. The real cause for this at the time was that I didn't know how to love myself. My grandfather's passing gave me the reason to stop taking drugs which was a major step for me as taking drugs wasn't part of the life I thought I would live. I did feel so much better giving up drugs but the label would not leave me as easy. I was trying to change my life, if I went on a night out there were always people taking drugs or people asking me to score drugs for them. I wanted to leave this behind but I just couldn't seem to get away from it. The relationship ended sometime in the early part of 2001. I felt so alone looking for an escape route and the answers to all my problems. I wanted to run away because I didn't know how to deal with my emotions. I will always remember my grandfather saying to me "Robert don't waste your lifetime down here, you have great potential and it's important for you to know this, no matter where you go in world, don't be an asshole, because you will always be guaranteed to meet one." On hearing his words playing in my mind, I wanted to change my life but didn't know how, what I did know was that I had to do something.

In April 2001 I lost my friend in a motorbike crash which was another major blow for me. It was also a major blow for my best friend Lee, who would be the last person to see our buddy Packie alive. I had been with him a couple of days beforehand. My whole family gathered around me, I was very volatile at the time but I managed to hang in there and battle through my pain. My best friend needed me as he was blaming himself. This could have been my end. I was really angry, loosing "Packie" was so hard, he was such a bright person with so much to live for, I was angry with something. I can't say it was God because I had only the church's teaching of what God was, an external power to be afraid of or obey and subject to others people beliefs "dogma".

This made me face my own mortality and made me think about life after we leave the earth. Either way, I thought I was dammed if I did and dammed if I didn't. I couldn't connect with these.

2

A Phone Call From America

I was at home one evening in early June 2001 and my phone rang. It was my long-time friend Neala who I hadn't spoken with for a while. We used to share a house with some friends in our home town. She had packed her bags and boarded a plane to New York.

We chatted away on the phone. "What are you doing with our life? Are you still partying?" She asked me. "No, I'm not. I'm not working full time at the moment and I've done partying. I want to move on with my life," I replied. "Well why don't you come and live in New York? It will be a fresh start. It's time to leave that part of your life behind you," she said. "How will I manage that? What will I do about a job or visa?" I asked. "Oh don't worry about that, that's minor detail. We can sort that when you get here. Everyone does. Come over on a holiday visa and see if you like it here. After all it is the land of opportunity. It's a no brainer to come and live here with me, it will be like old times," she said. I laughed down the phone. I was excited at the thought of this but I also felt great fear. However, at this particular time it was the only option I could see. I said yes and then started thinking of how I was going to pay for this? How will I get a job? When I get there—what will I do? I'm a welder by trade so I'm sure I will find something when I get there, it'll be fine. There was no planning and even less thought put into this move. It was my great escape, my golden ticket to the *Wonka factory*. It was my chance to change my life, get away from my past, start afresh and live the dream in the big apple. In the space of month or so I was boarding a plane to go and live in New York. I hadn't got much money to get me there. I had about seven hundred dollars in my pocket which was very little in the grand scheme of things. I wasn't really thinking ahead. Going to the states on a holiday visa finding a job, this was a spur of the moment decision, but I was escaping. It was exciting. My life was changing and starting to look up!

Before I was to leave for New York, my shoulders, back and neck seized up. I was in so much pain and I was saying to my mom that I didn't think I could go. Mom told me to try some pain killers which I did, but the pain was getting worse. It was like all the stress in world just hit me at once and my body decided it had enough. Whilst all this pain was going on, I was starting to think about my brothers and sister who I loved so much, especially my little brother Jason, the youngest by ten years. We had such a special friendship and bond as brothers. Some part of me knew that when I left, I would not see Jason as a child any more, he would be a man when I came home because I was planning to move to the U.S. and I knew it would be a very long time before I returned home.

The morning I was leaving my mom asked me "Are you able to fly? If you're that bad why won't you give our neighbour a shout, she does massage and healing?" "Healing, what do you mean?" I asked. "Just go down and ask and see what she can do to help you," answered my mother. I went down and knocked on the door and my neighbour answered. "Hello! I'm flying to America today and I've been in so much pain with my back and neck that I can't turn my head, can you help?" I asked. "I'm really sorry but I'm booked up for the next few days," she said. "Okay, thanks for your help," I said, turned around and started to walk down her drive. Just as I was about to walk out the gate she called after me "Robbie?" "Yes?" "Can you come back in an hour?" "Of course I can," I replied. "I will see you then, thank you".

My family and friends were coming and going from the house. My best friend Lee was there, we have been friends for the best part of our lives and have been through a lot of things together. Lee was such a great friend. He knew I hadn't much money so he gave me what little he had, "make sure you look after yourself. I will miss you and whatever you do, stay out of trouble," were his parting words. Knowing that our friendship meant so much, we were brothers forever. Mom and dad were very quiet which was unusual for them. Their way of trying to connect with me was by using a joke or some humour. Let's just say the skills weren't there to say "we love you." I most definitely hadn't the emotional skills to say I loved them both either, nor did I have any true meaning of the word love.

One hour later I went to my neighbour's house to get a message/healing. I went into the house feeling very apprehensive. "Make your way upstairs, turn right and go into the small room," she said. It would be what we would call the box room. "I will be with you in a minute," she added. I went upstairs and this conversation started again in my head. *What am I doing? What is this healing going to do? This is a load of crap!* On the other hand I was in so much pain I could hardly turn my neck. As I was having this conversation again in my head, she came into the room and said, "Now what's going on with you? How can I help?" I explained what was wrong. I got onto the specialized bed and she started to use some essential oils. I will never forget the heat from her hands. But for me at this time that's all it was—heat. An hour passed. I was half asleep when she said, "I'm finished." I thanked her greatly and left. Walking from her home I could feel instant relief, the heat was unreal. I was feeling so happy. America here I come! (The Angels were already helping; getting me prepared before I went to America. It's a pity I just wasn't awake to that at this time. My awakening is written on the stones of life, and it would be coming soon.)

At this time the blinkers were well and truly on for me and I had no understanding of how my life was going to change. The son, brother and friend that they would all see leaving the country would never be the same again. Saying goodbye was hard but not as hard as I thought because I needed to get away.

On the 3rd of August 2001 I landed at JFK airport. I've arrived! I will never forget that day. I was nervous going through immigration. *What if they check my bag?* My bag was packed to live in the states. I had packed winter cloths in the middle of summer. I had a lot of my personal stuff with me, like music, pictures and most of what I thought had meaning for me. So I was on a holiday visa but had my bags packed for a longer stay! Let's say that the summer I arrived the weather was so hot it was reaching 90/100 humidity.

The first week wasn't too bad. I was having a blast living in the boogie down Bronx, it was the most amazing place ever. I hadn't got the right clothes, that sucked, but it was a great adventure, a whole new life experience. I would travel into Manhattan to see Neala at her place of work which was a bar just off Time Square. I would take the subway which was an experience in itself! I had to start looking for work and this meant staying in the Bronx. So I would spend most days on my own. I would buy a phone card and ring home not wanting to be home, but afraid I was missing something.

Not working was hard and there were some other obstacles to overcome when I first got there. I had nowhere to stay, so I slept on Neala's floor or the chair in the house she was sharing with some other Irish guys. They didn't mind me staying there for a few nights, but I could start to feel the tension, that in itself was hard. I was feeling homesick and my money was running low. I was so afraid. I couldn't explain the fear I felt. I wasn't going home because I didn't want to be a failure, and I didn't want to go back to my old life. I really loved the American way and lifestyle, so going home was not an option for me. I was going to make this work no matter what. At this time I was going to be happy, feel like I belonged and nobody knew my past, so it was all good, a fresh start. I was always very independent, I liked my own company. I would consider myself prideful, as the old proverb says *pride comes before a fall*. My fall would come but not just yet.

I would get up every morning and stand at the food deli—Sean's deli. This is where all the lads would go to if they were looking for work. The different companies would pull up in their vans and ask lads to work. There could be quite a few lads waiting there, I just didn't seem to have success. Most jobs were for bricklayers and carpenters. Welders weren't on much demand. My confidence was getting a knocking. Each morning I was feeling like crap inside, not having the support of family or friends back home. This was getting me down, but as usual in my life, I put on a brave face and put on the mask to hide away what was really going on inside. Neala was there for me when she could, but she was working a lot of the time so maybe I hid how I was really feeling. Plus, I felt because she had family there, she didn't have to worry too much. If anything went wrong they were there for her. She did support me as best she could, what more could she do for me? Jobs weren't as easy to come by as she had thought they would be. I was losing hope and I was nearly out of money, so I phoned home. I spoke to my mom. I made out I was fine, but under that emotion I didn't say that I was finding it hard to find work. "Well, you will never guess what? I was talking to Jed, your old boss and I told him you were in New York. He said his brother is there," Mom said. Jed gave my mom his brother's name and number so I could ring him for some work. This was the best news ever! I was so happy!

The universe is always helping us most of the time we are just so asleep to its help

3

Stepping Outside My Comfort Zone

When Neala arrived home I told her the great news. Neala had some good news of her own, she had found us a new place to live. We were moving to east 235 street. It was a new apartment and we would be living in the basement. I was super excited! This meant I wouldn't have to sleep on the floor or the couch anymore. Things were starting to look up. "Are you going to ring that guy?" Neala asked. "Too right I am" I replied. So I phoned Ray and asked him if he had any work. "Are you a painter?" he asked. I said yes that I had done some painting before but not on a professional level. It was a white lie, but sure how would he know how foolish I was? Ray lived about 50 miles from me, a place called Terry town. He asked me if I drove here in New York and I told him I didn't. He said he was working on a job close to where I lived and he would pick me up in the morning. I was over the moon and so was Neala. Getting work was great news, a lifeline. I have always had a sense of feeling different, but how different still wasn't going to come to light yet. I've had some experiences from a child into my adult life, but my greater "knowing" wasn't there for me, it was all still very black and white. The Greatest part of me was so different, but I had not opened my "Pandora's box" to the universe and what was within. To express and understand life with such depth and knowing. At 9 am Ray called "Are you ready to work?" I was thinking hell yes "I'll be there in five minutes". I was feeling nervous. I thought to myself *will I be okay? I hope he doesn't see I'm not a pro, sure how bad can it be?* I met Ray who was so like his brother Jed, he was really down to earth. He asked me if I had ever worked with wood and varnish? I didn't answer at that stage. The house we were going to was very posh, so I thought to myself *just take your time you will be fine.* Ray explained that he had to go away for a bit. We arrived at the house which was stunning. This made me feel more nervous. I went inside and Ray set me up in the basement which had lovely wood with a bar and a pool table. Ray explained that my first job would be to varnish the wood. "Have you done this before?" he asked me. "Yes," I answered very reluctantly. "Start there, I'll be back in a while, I to have to get supplies," he instructed.

Oh God I was in for it. I started by lightly sanding the wood. I was used to sanding but the fun started when it was time to varnish. This had to be done to such a high quality finish and if I wish I knew then what I know now, thinning the varnish down was crucial making it easier to apply. I didn't know this so it was like glue; one dip of brush and the varnish went nowhere. I was frantically trying to spread the varnish, but not getting anywhere, so then I panicked. I decided to go to the windows where there was less wood, the obvious place and maybe "not". Well this was the ending for me. I was saying to myself *please something go right*, and next minute I'm getting varnish not only on the wood but the glass as well. I was now panicking; sweating, praying Ray wouldn't come back anytime soon. As soon as those thoughts went through my head all I could hear was Ray's voice "Robbie where are you?" he shouted. "I'm down here," I answered, my heart racing and my face as red as a beetroot. Ray walked in, took one look at me and said "Your some painter, are you finished this already?" In my head I'm saying *what do I say, do I say yes? This is my First day what if I get sacked?* Then Ray says "you've done really well, I'll finish here. There's rubbish and brushes that have to be cleaned up, you go up and look after that and take your time".

Call it whatever you like, but at this point without awareness, the universe was saying to me, "you're okay Robbie things will work out, we have a plan for you". I wasn't up to the standard to paint. Ray on some level definitely took pity on me and it was his kindness that got me through the next week or so. Even when he had no real work for me, he always found something to keep me going. Was luck in my favour? Were my angels looking after me? Or was I just being prepared for my real reason for being in America? I wasn't sure. Was I keeping me here, surviving just enough to reach my goal? Now remember, I'm still not really aware on my journey.

As I look back now I can see the glimmers of light that were shining for me and this is before what I would come to call *my true awakening*.

So I spent this short time working for Ray, knowing that I would have to look for something more permanent. Work was starting to dry up so I started looking for other jobs. We moved into our new apartment, I loved my new place and having my own space. But there was news to come. Neala arrived in one evening and told me she had a friend coming over. That's all I really knew at this time. I didn't mind too much. I was making new friends, there were a few lads living above us. They were all working and they said they would help me find some work. The best way to find a good job was to play Gaelic football. Now for me growing up I had no love for any kind of football, so this was going to be a challenge. The Lads got me a contact number for one of the football players. I phoned him and he asked me come training with them. I had to go out and buy boots and some stuff, but I have to say I have two left feet. Having grown up with a father who had managed every football team in my town and successfully helped bring them many winning cups, you would think I was going to be a football ace, but as I said before, I was blessed with two left feet. For me it was a case of "fake it till you make it." When one door closes another door opens. I started training with the team, they were all sound. "Are you working?" a guy asked me one evening. "No," I answered. "What kind of work do you do?" he proceeded. "I'm a welder," I replied. "Are you? One of the lads on the team might know someone looking for a welder, hold on and I will find out." He came back with a number and told me to ring them. Things were looking up. I made the phone call and got offered a job with this massive company as a welder. This was music to my ears. I'm still on my holiday visa and working, how crazy is that? The secret to getting a good job in the Bronx is to play football, the Irish version of which is called Gaelic GAA. I was starting to make some friends locally which definitely made life seem easier and getting a new job was just great. The hours were long but the money was great, it was a Win! Win! Win!

I was busy with my new job and life was good. Neala's friend was arriving soon. This girl came from the same town as me. Neala told me her friend was bringing a friend. I thought this was great, but was unaware that they would be moving in with us. The problem here was we lived in a two-bed apartment. I was working really hard as was Neala. I ask Neala "where are the girls going to stay?" "I was thinking your room, and you could take the living room" she replied. Well I was fuming and said I couldn't do this. I was getting up at 5 am and doing ten to twelve hour shifts a day to the pay rent and to live in a living room was not an option.

I wasn't going to do it. I've shared a room for most of my life and for me it was important to have my own space. Don't ask me why I was so hell bent on not giving up my room, but it just felt so right so me. The girls arrived and they didn't mind sharing the living room. We were all having such a ball, times were good but the clock was ticking. Little did we know that we were all going to have to face a decision that we never thought we would have to. This would be a moment in time that would change us all and one that would change the world forever. But before I bring you to this part of my journey, I'm going to rewind the clock back in time to this story I call ....

My Path, Before I Knew My Path
The Reading 1998

In order to go forward in life, sometimes we have to go back. I tell this story about my path before I woke up, this was an important part of my path and I can see that now. Showing me that Mother and Father God had always been with me, just like they are for you, but it's amazing how blind we can be.

I was roughly 19 when I went to see a fortune-teller with a friend. I can't remember my exact reasons for going to see this lady, she was an old lady who read from a deck of playing cards. We heard from other friends about this lady and I wanted to see what my future would hold. Was I going to be rich? Be happy? Own my own house? All the usual stuff.

When we arrived at the lady's home she opened the door. She reminded me of my grandmother. This would be my mom's mother. She said "Come in son". She showed me through to a bedroom and I took a seat at the edge of the bed. She shuffled her cards and started to read. She gave me a great smile and said "you have had a very traumatic life up to this point and I see so much pain and hurt around you. I have to tell you your mother loves you and always will. But your mother has gone through a lot of pain herself. Your immune system has suffered for many years, with chest infections and so on". This was so true I had suffered for a good part my life with these symptoms. "The reason for this is because you carry all the hurt and pain, not only from this lifetime but from others". Now at this point, I'm starting to judge because I had little understanding of past lives, never mind this one! The sceptic in me came out, or maybe this was a defence mechanism. The next thing I remember her saying was "you will go to America to get away from Ireland but you will never be the same man coming home Robert. You have a gift. You're a very powerful healer, but your fear will hold you back." I was saying in my own head *what a load of crap? I will never live in America! Gifted, what does that mean?* But at this time I was so out of touch, there wasn't a hope in the world of me seeing this. My reading was coming to an end and she said "Don't be afraid of your gifts, there will be many who will stand in your way, be jealous, or will not be able to understand you. In time they will see. Remember don't give up and one day you will be using your given gifts."

Sometime later I heard that some men broke into her home and robbed her. I will never understand the inhumanness. I had a deep feeling of sadness for this old lady, such a kind soul to have to go through this. What was her journey? Her words would play somewhere deep in my consciousness for many years that enabled me to see through the veils of darkness, to see our true divine light.

I can say now like anything else in life, when you look back, you don't always get to see the true value of life unless you are fully awake in the moment. Most people aren't and it's the inward journey that will bring you to the true value of your life and the meaning of what that is.

What is our life without meaning?
Who writes the rules we live in I ask again?

4

The Day the World Stood Still

(Song—*Peace on Earth* U2)

September-11-2001

To most people this date is when they remember where they were, what they were doing, or what they stopped doing.

I got up on the morning of September 11 and got ready for a normal day at work. For me this day felt a little different, but I can't explain what I felt inside. It was really calm, the sun was shining, it was going to be such a hot day. So I got dressed for work and I made my way down to Sean's deli to get my coffee and breakfast roll before I got picked up for work. Sean's deli is mad busy as usual at that time of the morning, vans and lads are coming and going. A lot of lads were making their way to different parts of the city to work. I was chatting to some of the lads I met most mornings, my van pulls up and off I go to the job. I arrive on the job and the bricklayers are already working. The Foreman of the job who's Irish came over to me and asked me to look after some jobs first thing. "Yes that's no problem, I'm just going to set up," I said. Now for some strange reason this morning I was getting ready, but it was taking me longer than usual. Not paying any attention to the time one of the lads came over "we're sending one of the lads to the shop to get some breakfast stuff, do you want anything?" he asked. "Yes can you get me a drink, a Gatorade or something?" I asked. I was setting up, but in the meantime I was up and down the stairs to the basement to take some measurements. There was a lorry bringing steel today that was needed and some other supplies. So I was working away and the foreman gave me a shout "your drink is here." It was roughly 8:20 am so we sat down; everyone was having a laugh. We were still waiting on the delivery so I asked the foreman "what time will the steel be here?" I was waiting on material. The time was 8:47 am. Everyone's phones started going crazy all of a sudden, there was something going on down town. The foreman called the driver, "I'm stuck mid-town, they're saying a small plane just hit the north tower of twin towers". The foreman said, "we have lads down that far, I will ring and see what they know." Everyone else was still working but talking about this plane. Now at this stage everyone's phones were going crazy, so we decided we would all chip in and buy a radio to hear what was happening at the towers.

When I think back about some of the lads giving out about having to chip in five dollars each to buy a radio I feel really annoyed, I know this sounds trivial but as people, we just don't think.

Some messages were getting through. It was a bigger plane that hit the north tower. Now I was starting to feel that something was not right here and some of the other lads were thinking the same. No one knew what to say or do. A small plane sounded bad, but then when word started coming back that it was a bigger plane, and word reaches us that most of the fire stations in the Bronx are now empty, this was a lot worse than we first thought. I was thinking *what's keeping the lad with the radio?* I looked at my watch it is 9:04 am. A call came through that another plane had just crashed into the south tower. I said "Oh My God." Everyone was panicking and didn't know what to do. My mind was racing, the fear I was feeling, the thoughts that started running through my mind *was this a world war? Am I going to see my family again?* I am filled with panic and fear. The lads were asking the foreman "what will we do, will we work on?" I went to my gang box and started to put stuff away. The foreman asked what I was doing? I replied "this is not right. I don't feel safe, and nobody knows what's really happening." He suggested that we wait and see. I really just felt this urge to go. I stopped putting away the stuff and I called it "I'm getting out of here. I'm going to make my way back to the Bronx. Don't worry about the tools, who's going to take them?" and with that everyone downed tools and we all left for our homes. Driving back there were people on the streets crying everywhere, it was so surreal this perfect day had just turned into hell and it was only the beginning. The smoke in the sky, the pure madness on the streets, it was like a

war zone. For many thousands of people it would be a day of such loss
and grief. For a lot more it was the beginning of the next part of our
evolution. When I arrived back to the Bronx I started seeing friends
and faces I knew on the street. I made my way back to my apartment
wondering if Neala was safe as she worked in the city. I went down
my stairs to see if all the girls were home. They were all there, I was
so happy. We were all in total shock. For me it's so hard to describe, it
was like being stuck in a Hollywood horror movie and at any minute
you were waiting to see the titles come up on the screen. I felt I was
stuck in this dreamlike state, feeling so numb and thinking of all those
poor people in the towers and the poor souls who were jumping to their
deaths and the whole world tuning in on their TV sets. Crazy! *Someone
wake me up please, is this real?* We were safe, but my thoughts were
with those people who were trapped in the buildings and the heroes
that were giving their lives unconditionally to save others, so many
forms of bravery happening.

In the middle of all this madness we were wondering if there were
any other attacks taking place and just then there was a news flash
"breaking news." Another plane crashed but this was into the Pentagon,
flight 77 at 9:37 am. I was feeling really worried because the media
were only showing what was happening in America. I felt we had no
connection to the rest of the world. Thinking *what else was happening
around the world, would I see my family again? Is this world war
three?* This is all I could think of and for that moment I had to try and
set aside all feelings that were not of love and any battles I had in the
past that had no meaning. It was just important to connect to my loved
ones again, to let them know I was safe, but also make sure they were
safe as well.

The phone in our apartment wouldn't call out, so I decided to make
my way back out on the streets to find a pay phone to ring home.
When I got down onto Katona Avenue there were queues to use the
pay phones. This was because of the influx of calls from cell phones,
so the networks went down that day. I joined the queue to phone home.
Waiting my turn its 9:58 am the first world trade centre crashed to the
ground. There was a great feeling of urgency to call home, to tell my

parents I was safe. Standing in the queue in total shock thinking mental thoughts, looking at people's faces crying, we were all over the place. I just couldn't believe this, who would attack America? This super power! The land of the free! I had always believed that this country was untouchable, the reality was that it wasn't. Bringing home that we're all so vulnerable and when you're in the thick and middle of it, there is always a reason for the moment. You are always where you are meant to be, there is no way to escape what your journey has chosen for you. It was at this moment of not having much belief I prayed to *GOD, please let me be safe*. What I have to explain though was my understanding in life: You pray to God only when you were in trouble or you did something wrong. Otherwise don't be wasting God's time. One of the reasons I felt totally separate from God was that I had little or no belief at this time. Somewhere deep, deep within, I had faith, finding that Faith wasn't to be found on the outside!

I was in the queue for the phone, it was 10:10 am and my turn came to make a call. I tried to phone home but I couldn't get through, it was about 3 pm Irish time and all phone lines seemed to be jammed. This day felt so unreal, and as I looked around the street I wasn't sure if this was the end, not getting through on the phone annoyed me, but there was little I could do. I decided to try again later. As I stood on the street talking to people, I heard all kinds of stories from people who had friends and family in the towers. What do you say? Hoping that they will be okay. I made my way back to our apartment. I arrived back at 10:25 am when this really bad feeling came over me. We were all looking at the TV and crash, there goes the second tower. I was feeling so numb and fighting back the tears. I knew this day my life and our world would change. It would never be same again and for me, it would be the starting event to point me towards my awakening, but I wasn't to know yet that my awakening was coming.

I finally got in contact with my family, the relief to hear their voices was fantastic. "I was so worried, we all were," mom said to me. She asked me what was I going to do? They thought it would be safer if I came home. I didn't know what I was going to do. I felt torn thinking *what's going to happen?* I wasn't sure but I had this deep feeling and desire to stay. My journey in the states wasn't at an end yet. I talked to my mom and said I would give it a few days to decide what to do, but first I had to chat to Neala and see what she was going to do. In the immediate aftermath, every TV station just replayed 911. For me it was becoming ground hog day. I was becoming so numb to it all. I decided that I wasn't going to watch TV. I felt the pain of all the people hurting in my heart. The media were just war mongering and that was so scary. The people were so angry, so much hurt and pain—I could see and feel this. *Why was I going through this? Why am I feeling so sensitive to people's pain again?* I can't understand. My mind felt so clouded. I was so sensitive to a lot of things at this time. The feelings I experienced were very like my childhood. I hadn't the got tools to express how I felt, so I did what I always did, suppressed my feelings. I hid away and continued with life, ploughing my way through it. I buried my head and just moved forward. Things were really hard, not just for me but also for the girls I lived with and the people of New York. I wasn't too sure if I would stay or if I would go back home. The feeling of being a failure wasn't long creeping in and going home then wasn't an option for me. My pride "Ego" was doing all the talking and I felt that I had no choice but to stay. Going back to Ireland, I felt I would have no life or meaning.

I spoke with Neala and asked her "what are we going to do?" Neala was also unsure what to do, but I knew in my heart she didn't want to go home. I was back working and for me this took my mind away from what was going on in the world. I started using drink as a way of escapism, a crutch, my way of hiding so many feelings and emotions. The sticky plaster syndrome: stick a plaster on the problem to cover the cuts and bruises, but eventually in the end, the plaster will fall off and the true wounds will be revealed. We're all trying to get our lives back to normal, but with four of us in a two bed apartment things felt very claustrophobic. Growing up sharing a room with two brothers, I was used to having people around, but it was starting to get a little hard for me. With my male energy and three female energies, there was bound to be different opinions and feelings. I tried my best to work through this but inside I felt like I was a kettle coming to the boil, but I kept a brave face on to avoid any arguments. The conversation with Neala came up again, were we going to stay or go? We both decided then and there that we would stay. For me when I made this decision that was it. I was going to make a life here and find all the happiness I had been looking for. It's a tough place to live, but if you're a fighter you can survive.

It was Friday, payday. I was feeling good and I was going places. It was coming close to the end of the evening, pay time! The way we got paid was like something you would see in a black comedy movie. The boss would come in with a huge bag of cash. He would sit in the corner with the foreman, your name would be called and when you went over the bag was opened and you were handed an envelope stuffed with cash. This was such an amazing feeling. I was on top of the world and it felt like my life had a flow to it. So as my name was called I went over to the boss and foreman. As he paid me he asked me if I would be interested in working on the Saturday and Sunday for him. (This was not a question!) He emphasized how important this job was and told me I would be paid well. So of course I said yes, there was a bit fear around my boss. I was also a "people pleaser" and didn't want to let him down. I will never forget him saying to me "don't let me down, I'm really relying on you Robbie so don't go on the beer. I have a lot of men coming tomorrow and it's so important that you are here." This man didn't give you a verbal sacking. It was more of a physical one if you let him down and I knew this to be so true. There was no way in the world I was going to let him down, or so I thought! I had been paid, it was close to the end of our working day and those who were working Saturday and Sunday could go home. So we packed up our gear. I jumped into the van with the lads and headed back to the Bronx. The vans would drop us off in a place called MacLean Avenue and there were quite a lot of pubs there. I had all the intentions of going home but some of the lads that were going for drinks asked me to join them. I had initially said no as I was working the next day, but they were very insistent that I come along. They were a friendly bunch of lads so I agreed to go for a bottle and I also wanted to be part of the peer group.

It was around 5 pm "sure one or two bottles won't do any harm."
I thought I would be home about 6:30 pm, which turned into 9 pm
and before I knew it the time was after 11 pm. At this point you can
imagine the state I was in. But the lads kept buying rounds and I kept
knocking them back as you do when you have a 5 am start! It was
roughly 3 am when I arrived back in my apartment. Neala was very
annoyed with me for being in such a state. She was only looking out
for me, worrying about work. I reassured her that I would be fine. I
went to bed and about twenty minutes later I started to feel very ill,
without warning I was violently sick. Now I'm not the biggest drinker
in the world so it could have been alcohol poisoning. I slept through
the alarm as I was so comatose from the drink and lack of sleep.
Because I felt so sick, I wallowed in my own self-pity, but also felt
depressed from drinking and guilt ridden for not turning up for work.
What have I done? I had landed this great job, made a promise to the
boss and let him down. I spent all that day in bed and slept through
to Sunday. But instead of biting the bullet and getting up for work on
Sunday, I couldn't do it. I was in so much fear about the silly mistake
I had made. I was beating myself up so much that the Sunday led to
Monday and then Tuesday. At this point I was completely and utterly
in a place where I didn't know how to get out of. Neala started to
ask questions about my absence from work. The pressure from this
lay heavily on my shoulders and I didn't know how to tell her the
reason I didn't turn up for work was because of my night on the beer.
Even though she probably knew. Neala tried to persuade me to ring
my boss and see if I could return to work. I couldn't do this as I was
just too afraid to. I can now say I know that the fear that I felt then
came from my childhood fears. There was a part of me that lost this
communication. I didn't know how to communicate, it's so hard to
explain what was going on inside but I had to get myself out of this.
I hadn't left the house for those four days, and on the Wednesday
morning I plucked up the courage to go down to the Sean's Deli, in my
head I'm saying "please don't let me meet any of the lads or bosses
from work". Walking down towards the deli I buried my head between
my shoulders in case I met anyone I knew. There was a part of me

saying *if I meet anyone, ground open up and swallow me please.* I'm in the Deli, standing in the queue talking to a couple of the lads and the next minute I heard the door opening. I looked behind it was the foreman. The blood just drained out of me and I could feel my knees knocking, my heart was pounding. As I plucked up the courage with this whimper in my voice to say hello to him, he gave me such a dirty look and completely ignored me. Now at this point I wished I was six feet under. I paid for my food and I started to make my way back to the apartment. Out of nowhere I had this conversation in my head "go back down talk with him, at least apologize." So I turned on my heels and went back down, not knowing what I was going to say. As I came around the corner, the foreman was coming out of the deli. I went up to him and just as I was about to speak, he started to shout at me "You let us all down Robbie, why didn't you turn up for work? You knew you weren't going to come in, why didn't you just ring? We all felt so let down by you Robbie, plus we had to ring someone else to come in and do your job." I was just standing there feeling so bad inside I really felt like crying, beating myself up inside for the last four days knowing I had let myself down. "I'm sorry" I said. "Sorry just doesn't cut the mustard around here," he replied. He could see my eyes welling up and I also feel that he knew I wasn't a bad person, that I was a hard worker and I had just made a mistake.

"Those lads that you had drinks with turned up for work, they are seasoned drinkers and you're a good lad but don't get caught up in that way of life here. I've seen so many lads come over from Ireland and do the same," he told me. He was giving me some good advice and inside I knew that this was my truth. "We all make mistakes, I will make a phone call but I can't promise you anything. Be at the deli tomorrow morning, be ready for work, but I can't say if I will have work for you," he continued. "Thank you," I said and again I apologized for letting them down. "I will see you in the morning".

I went home and I never slept a wink that night with worry. I tossed and turned, my mind was racing and my heart was pounding. Why do we do this to ourselves? Or choose this experience in our lives? It's horrible, but this seems to be something we put ourselves through. The

next morning arrived and I made my way to the deli. The van pulled up
and boys asked me to jump in. I was delighted. I arrived at work and I
was waiting for the boss to come in but I had my guard up. It was never
my intention to miss work or let the company down. This was just a
cycle that was going on in my life and I couldn't or hadn't the tools to
break it. I have worked in so many jobs throughout my life, but could
never seem to find the perfect balance. I have always felt like I had
more to offer and there was more to me, but I hadn't got the know how
to explore this fully. I felt that a lot of this came from my childhood
into young adulthood. I was down in the basement welding some steel
and working away when suddenly I stopped, I lifted my welding shield
and there he was, the boss—nickname "mental" because of his temper.
Well the blood just drained out of me. He was walking towards me and
the look on his face was on of pure rage. At this point I'm saying in my
head *oh please God get me out of this, I promise I won't mess up again.
Please! I swear*! Why do we do this to ourselves? Repeating cycles?
What's the reason? He walked right up to me and gave me a warning
look and walked right past me. I felt relief straight away but was still
waiting for him to attack or pounce. I heard the stories of how he had
sacked other lads and they were only late! And here I am costing him
money. Just as I'm thinking this he walked back over to me and I was
thinking *this is it, I'm gone* and next he said "Oh you decided to turn up
did you?" "Yes" I said with a look of terror on my face. I was just about
to grovel when he said "you let me down and the lads that turned up for
work. Drink can be the ruination of any man. You're a good chap and
a hard worker, this will be your first and last chance with me, so keep
your head down and go back to work. Oh and by the way, it took a lot
courage to come back to work," and with that he was gone. Relief! I felt
it was like all my Christmas's came at once. I felt so much better at that
moment, my life was back on track and I still had a job. Even though I
was only on a holiday visa and shouldn't be working, but for me it was
the only way I could see forward. So as the weeks passed I began to
think of home a lot, really missing my family, friends, and feeling so
lonely. I just kept my head down trying to look ahead in a positive way.

Winnie the Who? Will the Real Tigger Please Stand Up!

It was October and I was getting ready for Halloween. There was going to be a fancy dress party at one of the local bars. I was really looking forward to getting a costume and I was looking at a Tigger costume at the Disney store. It was amazing, I'd never seen anything like it. Time was ticking away and soon Halloween came. I bought my Tigger costume to go to the fancy dress party. I was so excited! It was my first Halloween in New York and I just loved the effort that people were putting in for the occasion, there was a real buzz in the air. Rob, Neala's boyfriend was dressed up as Winnie the Pooh. When we arrived at the fancy dress there was another guy dressed as "Tigger" there. The other Tigger kept coming over saying "c'mon." Then, out of nowhere he hit me a punch in the stomach and a fight broke out between the other Tigger and me. He was lead to the door and escorted outside! Picture that .... I didn't know being a Tigger would be so territorial, but there you go! America was growing on me day by day and for the first time in my life I had this feeling of being in the right place at the right time as the city had just so much to offer. I was working really long hours but I was making a few dollars. This is just the way of life in America and you either loved it or hated it. It had this magnetic hold on me and without realising it at the time, the reading I had all those years ago with the old lady had happened. I was living the dream the American dream, like so many before me had done and so many after will do.

There was still an air of hostility in America and a lot of talk about wars and terrorists, we were still under high alert and threat of attack. Lower Manhattan, which had now become ground zero had their own battles looking for survivors, or at least the remains for the families so they could get closure. This would prove painstakingly slow as there was so much rubble and debris to work through. I remember travelling down town to lower Manhattan and when you got close to where the world trade centres were, you could get the smell of burnt rubble and this feeling was vary eerie plus seeing the tributes and all the pictures of the people who lost their lives really affected me. Even

writing about this at this moment, I feel a great wave of emotion for
that time. There was the threat of a chemical warfare and anthrax
would soon be the word that was in everybody's mind. There was just
so much uncertainty for everyone. I could feel this change in my life
and for many more there was a wave of change happening in the world.
America is a special place to me and such a magical place, but the
threat of anthrax was very real and scary and the media totally played
to the note of fear. The world we were living in was making a change
and it was the beginning of this war on terror. *If America is not safe
where is?* It was like this was the driving force for the fear.

For me it was just a matter of keeping my head down and moving
forward. After all I'm Irish and this was something we had done
through many generations.

It was kind of weird, I was in the states on a holiday visa, I was
working and thinking of staying. The weeks were passing and I was
coming close to my visa running out. After 9/11, security was stepped
up and there were a number of more raids by immigration officers
on building sites, homes and bars. We were all hearing horror stories
about people getting caught and sent home with a 5 or 10 year ban. I
spoke to Neala, we had so much to think about. Neala travelled to the
bar she worked in off Time Square every day. Police and immigration
were now stopping people on trains and buses. It's a funny place to find
yourself in. I never went to the states to break the law, but I was just
about to. To go home at this point wasn't an option, fight or flight and
my choice would be?

5

Treading the Thin Line

November 4—2001

My three-month visa was on its last days and I knew talking to Neala would help me make my choice a lot easier. From the next day I would be classed as an illegal alien and I would have to be so much more careful. What must I have been thinking of? This meant no bank accounts, no driver licence and no real medical care. Everything was cash. The reality was there was no going home, the choice was made. The dye was cast!

Christmas was fast approaching and we were all getting in the holiday mood. Neala was going to cook Christmas dinner and I was really looking forward to some good home cooking. It was snowing and the weather was pretty harsh. It was my first time where there was snow for more than a couple weeks, and at the beginning it was fun having to dig yourself out of the snow! It wasn't long before it lost its magic. Don't get me wrong I like the snow but I am not a massive lover of it. I am a sun child born in mid-summer. It was such an amazing sight to see all the Christmas lights and how people decorated their homes. 5th avenue is just amazing and you see the world-famous Ice Rink at the Rockefeller Center, which has become a quintessential New York City winter. It has a fairy tale feeling to it which brings out the inner child in people.

Christmas day arrived and I was looking forward to dinner with Neala and her boyfriend Rob and calling my family to wish them a happy Christmas. This is a big day for our family in Ireland. Everyone would go to our grandmothers. The adults would play cards and all the grandchildren would be there with whatever Santa brought them, a great occasion. I don't know how my grandmother coped with so many grandkids running around, but then again, my granny has the patience of a saint! What an amazing lady and a faith so strong. She prayed for everyone in the family. We always say her prayers would be heard throughout heaven, a very wise lady.

Neala was cooking, I opened a beer and we exchanged presents. I phoned home and I was chatting to mom. I asked "How's Jason, Joey and Vicky?" "They're good" she replied. "How's dad? Is he gone to work?" My dad drove a taxi and would always work on Christmas day after dinner. Neala shouted in "Ask your mom how to speed up the roast potatoes?" As I'm having this conversation I realise how much I miss my mom's Christmas dinner. My mom is an amazing cook. She instructed Neala to baste a small drizzle of oil over the roast potatoes and to turn the oven a little higher. We had been getting this funny smell in the apartment for few days beforehand but we really didn't think too much about it, how silly of us! I was chatting away to mom when I heard a huge bang followed by a scream. Just then Neala goes running past my bedroom door at ninety mile an hour screaming. I say to mom "I have to go." I went to the kitchen and our cooker was on fire. Rob, Neala's boyfriend was there with a tea towel trying to put out the flames that were spreading around our kitchen. Neala had done as asked and turned the oven up. She had asked Rob to check on the meat and potatoes. What we didn't know at the time was that there was a gas leak at the back of the oven. The flames had built up inside. As Rob opened the oven door the build-up went boom! And he went flying. Neala panicked and ran upstairs to get help. I can still hear her screaming in my own mind. It wasn't funny at the time, but funny to look back on. We got the fire sorted but let's just say Christmas dinner was off the menu, my first Christmas in New York and it went out with a boom!

New Years' eve arrived and Neala was going away which meant I was home alone. I decided to have a few beers and celebrate. This was my first new year's eve away from home and my first in New York. I should have been out partying but I was alone and feeling so lonely. I started thinking about my life and where it was going. I was really trying to find my sense of purpose. I really felt so isolated with only my dark thoughts to creep into my mind. I was here in my apartment when most of the people I knew had plans, for me this was the start of the feeling of not wanting to live. *What is wrong me?* I asked myself. Feeling so lonely and isolated, all these emotions were hitting me all at once. I came here to find happiness but felt like crap inside and all I wanted to do was to take my own life. So lost inside, angry and feeling like my life had no meaning. There was a battle going on in my mind, one-half saying "do it—take your life" and the other giving me every reason not to. I had been trying to suppress these feelings and put them back into the dark hole where they had come from and continue life as if it was perfect, always smiling on the outside but inside in complete turmoil, asking "Why has this wave of great sadness come over me? What is wrong with me?" As I asked myself this question, I start to cry thinking "I hate myself" and the feeling of guilt was overwhelming. I went to the bathroom and as I looked into the mirror, I asked myself "Who am I? What am I? Why do I hate myself? Why is this place I find myself in so painful?"

6

The Mirror

(Song—*Man in the mirror* Michael Jackson)

I was looking into the mirror at this person looking back at me. I
didn't recognise him! I was crying, when I started to feel this presence
around me like I felt when I was a child. As I felt the energy of this
presence with me again I didn't fully understand it, but the feeling of
wanting to kill myself wasn't as strong. I knew there was someone or
something comforting me at that time. I started to feel at ease and the
dark thoughts slipped away. I was still crying, looking at myself, the
person in the mirror, trying to understand why I thought these thoughts
and felt this way. I asked myself again "what's wrong with me?" As I
looked into my reddened eyes, I felt this polar shift and my whole body
felt lighter, in the next moment I was brought back to a time. Yes! I was
taken out of my body back to a time when I was taking drugs in my
local nightclub. I saw myself taking drugs in the nightclub, at a rave.
As I looked around, I started to see all the people I would party with
back in the day, the nightclub was full. Everybody was spaced out of
their minds on drugs. I was with my friends in a part of my life where
I was lost, searching to find who I was in that time. I couldn't see this
as the drugs had a great way of hiding all the demons and this made it
harder to find the part of me I was so longing for. I saw myself walking
to the dance floor, everybody was bouncing around. I knew most of
the people on the dance floor. I started to dance and I felt amazing!
My body felt so alive. Some guy on the dance floor asked me if I want
a 'rush'. A rush is a term that people used to get themselves higher,
there are different types of rushes. The best way I can explain this is
that a person cuts off your blood supply and you hold your breath for
about 30 seconds, they pick you up and slam you to the floor giving
you a rush of blood to the head, getting you so high your brain would
feel like it is going to explode. The guy asked me again if I wanted one

I said "no, I'm feeling really high." "Are you sure? He asked. I never answered him. A few minutes later he came back, nagging me, saying, "come on, have one you will love it".

I gave in and said "don't give me a big rush. I'm feeling a little out of it and don't let me go!" This guy was really strong and started to give me the rush. I said again "don't let me go" next thing he picked me up and slammed me down. I wasn't ready or in a good place, but he let me go anyway. I blacked out, when my feet hit the floor he let go. I fell straight to the floor and smashed my face into the dance floor. I was gone, knocked out. I left my body for a brief few moments and could see everyone standing around me. I was looking on at myself as I lay on the dance floor. I was also seeing a massive bright light and this was no disco light. People were starting to gather around me and as I came through, the first face I saw was a girl from my school days, the look on her face was one of sheer terror as she looked at me. "Are you okay?" she asked. It looked like she was saying it in slow motion, and as she pointed to my face I could see a lot of blood but had no idea it was mine. As I tried to leave the dance floor, people started running over to me, saying "are you okay? Look at your face!" I couldn't understand what they were saying so then someone said "Get lee." Lee is my best friend since first class in school. I heard someone say "He needs to go to hospital." I went to the gents to clean myself up. I was standing in front of the mirror looking at my bloody face and thinking to myself *what have I done to myself now?* I was completely sober and lucid at this point. I had so many thoughts running through my mind, worrying about how I was to explain this to my parents and on top of this, the shame I felt was overwhelming. I took a seat outside the gents and someone brought me water and a tissue. I was not in any pain but I was feeling very shocked and thinking *why did I allow this insanity to happen to me?* In this instant I could see everything so clearly, and with that came a very real and sane moment. I started looking around the nightclub and began to see bright coloured lights emulating hovering around people, they looked like they were hugging them, keeping them safe. But it took this massive shock for me to see again what I had been seeing as a child, just for that brief moment. When they weren't hovering they were moving fairly fast between other people. I could see all these different colours around people, some had shapes and others had not.

The colours I was seeing were unimaginable! They were so beautiful and when they came closer to me they moved slowly and weren't as transparent as when they were moving away, when they moved really fast. I was looking really hard into my eyes, the next thing all I heard were lots of loud bangs! It was the fireworks outside. I was back in my apartment and I was looking at the man in the mirror. The Angels were now beginning to enter back into my life.

It was early January and I couldn't help thinking about what I had experienced on New Year's Eve, but the fear crept in again just like it did when I was a child.

I suppressed what had happened as I didn't know how to deal with the reality, so I locked it away deep within my mind in a place that wouldn't be easy to reach. This was because I was afraid to face my real truth, which was that I had always been connected to my Angels. The feelings brought things up making me look deep inside and still question my existence. January was a very quiet month work wise and I was starting to worry about money. We were moving to a bigger apartment on the same street, just a few doors away and the rent was a lot more expensive, so I felt the pressure. The new apartment was lovely. The only downfall was the landlord and his family lived underneath us and that would have its own complications. Before we moved in they wanted our passports to take a photocopy of and I remember saying to Neala "I'm not giving it to them. We will be handed over to immigration if anything goes wrong." "Don't be silly Robbie, they won't know you're not meant to be here," Neala said. I remember saying to myself that all they have to do is read our visa waiver on the passport and we were "gonners." But I did trust Neala and she was very good at making me feel at ease. I started a new welding job, it was hard work with long hours, all of the things I was used to. Life was starting to look up again! But it was the age old question again in the back of my mind *would I ever find a job that I would fit and be happy?*

I started dating a girl called Kim in February 2002. She was like a breath of fresh air to me and great fun to be with. Kim was of American and Irish descent and came from a good family. She was a well-educated and an ambitious girl who worked for a financial company. The first few weeks with Kim were quite challenging as I had to tell a white lie about my residency saying I had a visa. I was afraid that by me being illegal it would affect our relationship. I wanted Kim to get to know me before I said what my true status was. I was working at the time so Kim didn't have a reason to question me. I have to say this was such an amazing time for me and everything was perfect; we were living the dream together.

I would travel into the city most nights to see Kim. She lived mid-town in a beautiful high-rise apartment. It was such an exciting time in my life. She was such a kind and caring person and this would always shine through her. I remember having some issues getting my wages. Kim thought it was strange that I got paid in cash and was asking me lots of questions. She was onto me big time! I knew I would have to tell her the truth at some stage but I kept putting it off, afraid that she would run a mile. When we eventually had the conversation, she laughed, "I knew all along Robbie!"

When I worked in the city I would travel home on the subway and then get a bus back up to the Bronx 235th. Some days I would stop for a few drinks in a pub called the Catalfo. As we would we say back in Ireland, it was a real spit-on-the-floor pub with the odd fight or two! I played pool and I enjoyed the craic. I befriended a lovely chap called John in this pub. It's funny how the universe sends you people or things as you need them without you even knowing the reason why. So, over the next couple weeks I popped in for a few drinks after work. The Irish pubs in the Bronx offered free dinners to get the lads in drinking and it was definitely better than making dinner yourself after working a 12 hour shift!

I met John most days. We would buy rounds of drink for one another, play games of pool and put the world to right with our conversations! John was born in Ireland himself but his family had emigrated to America when he was a child, so we had lots of stuff in common.

We would talk about the 'old country', as he liked to call it. We were getting on great, he felt like a big brother to me. The more I got to know and trust John the more comfortable I felt sharing my story with him. I remember Kim warning me at the time to be careful as you never know whom you're speaking with. Never was a truer word spoken!

Without listening to Kim's advice and with the help of a few pints my tongue was lose and my guard was down! Before I knew it I was telling John some home truths that I was illegal and working. I wasn't proud of it. John was listening and not saying much. As John headed to the restroom the bar person came over to me and said "I couldn't help but hear what you were saying to John about you being illegal. Do you realise he's a cop, a detective for the NYPD?" I nearly joined John in the restroom with the shock of hearing this. I never thought to ask John what he did for a living, I just presumed he was a builder or something. I never questioned why none of the lads sat with him. He was so quiet this guy "there is no way he could ever be a cop," I said to the bar person. "I'm telling you he is, be careful, I'm only looking out for you," he replied. "What other person would be allowed to carry a gun into a pub? Look at his hip when he comes out from the restroom," the bar person continued. I couldn't believe this. I was in shock. Before I knew it, the restroom door opened. John came back to his seat beside me and as he sat down I got a glimpse of his gun. I was trying to put on a brave face but in my head I was thinking of doing a 'Forest Gump' and running like I'd never ran before! John was chatting as normal. I on the other hand was having a complete meltdown, waiting for my chance to bolt out the door! My mind was racing with thoughts that I would be arrested at my home because I stupidly told John my address! So as John made his way over to the jukebox, I saw my opportunity to bolt out the door. When I arrived back at my apartment breathless, I told the girls what had just happened. They didn't seem to be too bothered. I on the other hand was freaking out so I went to stay with Kim for a few nights.

I packed up a bag and headed into the city to Kim's as this would be a welcome distraction. Even though we were both worried about me getting found out and the possibility of me getting deported, we decided to make the most of our time together and have some fun! When I stayed with Kim I felt so good inside. I felt so happy that we got on so well together.

After staying at Kim's for a few days I had to go back home to the Bronx to get some stuff for work. As I made my way past the deli to my apartment fate intervened and I bumped into John! I had nowhere to run and hide. I no choice—I had to speak to John. "What happened to you the other day?" he asked. "I went to put music on and when I turned around you were gone. I thought I had done something to you. Is everything okay?" "Yes, I'm fine," I nervously replied.

John went onto to tell me that the people behind the bar told him that they had warned me he was a cop. I confided that I panicked and thought he was going to hand me in. John laughed and said he understood my situation, he was my friend and not to worry. John echoed Kim's advice about being careful about what I said to some people. This was a big lesson for me because I'm such an open and trusting person I presumed that everyone would be the same. "Now let's go for bottle buddy," John suggested. I was so relieved to hear those words. John would later open up and confide in me the reasons he never told me he was a cop. John was struggling with the loss of his brothers after 911. The trauma of 911 left great scars on his heart and mind. John was such a strong man yet the pain he was going through was immeasurable.

John phoned me one day and asked if I could come and see him at his apartment—he had something for me. I spent the day wondering what John had for me. I was so curious and couldn't wait to find out what it was so I called straight after work that same day. When I arrived at John's apartment he was so happy to see me, giving me the guided tour of his apartment. He loved to play the drums and had an electronic set, which I had never seen before. John said to me "I want to give you this card, it's called NYC PBA card (Patrolmen's Benevolent Association). We only get a few each year to give to our family members. You can use it if you ever get into trouble, it will help you. If anyone asks where you got it just say my name, where I work,

the department and you will be okay. Oh and say you're my cousin."
I was speechless at this point. I had heard about these special cards
before. One of the guys I worked with had one. He said it was so hard
to get the card as only close family members were allowed them. This
guy told me he got stopped for speeding once and when he produced
this card his speeding offence was automatically quashed. He said it
was like his get-out-of-jail card.

When John handed me the card I realised it was a special edition
PBA September 11th Card which had even more meaning and value. I
was so grateful. I thanked him for this thoughtfulness and for looking
out for me. Things always happen for a reason. You always meet the
right people at the right time. Divine timing!

Hard Decisions & Life Changing Choices

We started a new job in midtown in an army barracks which was also
a museum. We had to be on site for a set time as we had to get security
clearance. If you were late and missed the time you wouldn't be
permitted on the site. Missing a day's wages wasn't an option! It was
some set up because we were nearly all illegal, yet we were working in
a government building!

Once we got clearance we went onto the roof and worked there until
the shift ended. It was the dirtiest job ever! We had to replace all the
fire escapes throughout the building. The weather was getting good
as we were heading for summer so it was pretty hot up on that roof. I
had two labourers helping me who were brothers from Guatemala. The
connection they had together reminded me of my own two brothers
back home in Ireland who I missed greatly. They were such hard
workers. I was mostly welding whilst the boys were grinding out the
old steel for the new steel to be replaced.

Most Mexican lads working on sites weren't treated very well. I
helped them a lot more than the other lads did. I really felt for these
two brothers. They were so happy but the odd time when I looked into
their eyes I could see a great sadness.

Like me, these two brothers were living and working in America illegally. One day I decided to ask them why they chose America to live and work. They told me that back home they were so poor, they could barely feed themselves and there was little to no employment. They felt like they had no choice but to try to come to America because their life was so hard. They had my full attention whilst they were telling me their story. They told me that they had another brother. All three of them walked for four weeks sharing one pair of trainer's to get to the border. "Where is your other brother working?" I asked. What they would tell me next was the saddest story I had ever heard. Their other brother died as they were walking to America. They had to make the hardest decision that anyone would ever have to make and leave their brother behind. If they turned and started to walk home with their brother's body they may not have made it home alive themselves. So they made the difficult decision to continue on their journey to America. I was in complete shock at hearing this horrific story, my heart felt so sad. I couldn't imagine having to do this with my own brothers. I felt so grateful and lucky that day for my own family and how much I loved them.

This tragic story really made me look at myself and question my purpose in this world. I asked myself *what am I doing? What is my purpose?* Somewhere deep inside I was looking for answers, but I was not awake to receive the understanding or answers I needed at this time.

My daydream was quickly interrupted with the sound of the grinder. The brothers were grinding and preparing the metal for me. They would never wear masks, which I thought was crazy. I was giving them a hand to grind the metal to speed things up. I had run out of dust masks so I was completely exposed to the fumes and dust from the abrasive wheel and metal. What I didn't realise at the time was that the original paint on the old fire escapes was a lead based paint which is not very good for your health, especially when it heats up with a grinder and you're breathing in the dark blue smoke that escapes from it. This smoke could cause lead poisoning in the blood. I could feel and taste the smoke and fumes. Thank goodness I was only doing this for a day, the brothers were doing this for a week or so.

When we finished that day I asked the brothers why they had no masks to wear. They said they were afraid to ask the boss in case they lost their jobs. I couldn't believe it. I thought this was complete madness. I knew right there and then that I would have to do something about this. I headed over to Kim's apartment after work. I felt ill as I travelled on the subway to Kim's. I had the most awful taste in my mouth. When I arrived at Kim's I sank into the sofa still feeling very unwell. Kim rang her father for advice. Her father thought it sounded like a touch of lead poisoning. All I could think about was the two brothers. I had to do something about this. I phoned my boss straight away. There was an exchange of a few words. However, when I explained everything to him he said he would have all the proper gear sorted for the next day. Result! I was delighted.

7

Better to Be Born Lucky Than Rich

I woke up very early the next morning. My stomach was sick all night so I was considering phoning work to say I couldn't make it. When I called my boss he threatened me with the sack if I didn't show up for work. It was a dog-eat-dog. I didn't want to lose my job and when I told Kim she was disapproving so I got ready for work in a rush so I wouldn't be late!

Take your time; you will arrive when you arrive!

I was in a panic to get to work on time for the security check. I was running to get to the sub way station 86th on Lexington. Just as I was about to go down the stairs I felt a very strong presence around me, it felt like a warning. I didn't stop to think or question this feeling. As I reached the platform I noticed all the ticket stalls were packed with huge queues for each one. I looked at my watch to see the time when I heard a voice softly in my ear saying "Robbie slow down. Take your time. You will arrive when you arrive." I never even blinked. Instead I questioned why on earth was I telling myself to slow down? This was me reasoning with my mind and still not awake or fully listening. I made my way to the queue for my train and before I knew it I heard my train coming. I needed to get this train in order to get to work on time. I heard the bell for the doors opening: ding dong. Then I had a complete moment of madness. I saw an opportunity to get through the gate used for wheel chairs and buggies. I dashed over to the gate, bolted through it and onto the train. *Oh my God, what am I after doing?* My heart was pounding out of my chest. The train was packed so I had to stand. I had a bag with me with a change of clothes in it. I heard the sound of the door closing: ding dong. As the train started to pull off I had a real sense of relief knowing I had gotten onto the train and would arrive to work on time, or so I thought!

Famous Last Words

Whilst I was standing in the centre of the train carriage I felt the same strong presence around me that I felt at the top of the stairs at the train station. I felt like I was being warned about something. Before I had time to even think about this I felt a hand on my shoulder. I turned around and there was a man holding onto my top. I was just about to say "What do you think you're at?" and push his hand away when I saw him reach around his neck and pull his police badge! *Oh no* I thought to myself. "I'm a Transit Officer. I followed you onto to the train at Lexington Avenue. I'm arresting you for not paying to get onto this train. There is fine of 500 hundred dollars with a possible jail sentence. The city of New York doesn't take kindly to these offences," were his words to me. He handcuffed me and explained that he was taking me down town into Central Police Station. I was totally bricking it. Everyone on the train was looking at me like I was a terrorist. The shame and embarrassment was unbearable.

We got off the train at 68th street, Hunter College. As the doors opened: ding dong, he was on his radio saying, "central send a car to pick up at Hunter College." At this point all I could think of was being sent home and getting into trouble for being illegal. My mind was going crazy. What about Kim and all my belongings in my apartment? When things like this happen they never bring you home to get your stuff, they lock you up, get you on the next available flight and deport you out of the country.

My thoughts were running wild ... *what if they go to my apartment and catch the girls?* So I made a decision right there and then that I would not give my real address. The cop was really annoyed and angry with me saying he was sick of people like me wasting his time when he could be doing more important jobs. As I listened to him giving out I was beating myself up inside. "How stupid am I? I'm getting what I deserve for not being honest." My parents always taught me to be honest—I was brought up with good morals.

We left the train platform and the cop pointed me towards the street holding me by my handcuffs behind my back. We got up onto the street and he asked me some questions. "Why did you do that? Have you got ID on you? What's in the bag? Why were you in such a rush?" I didn't know what to say. I was speechless. The police car pulled up to take me to the station. I started shaking at this point. "What's your name? Have you got ID?" he asked. "I have ID in my back pocket, in my wallet," I replied. The ID I was carrying came from my local police station in Ireland. It is an offence not to carry ID in the state of New York. So he got my wallet and the questions started again. "Where were you coming from this morning?" "My girlfriend's apartment," I answered. "Where were you going to?" he asked. Not thinking straight I said "To the Bronx to visit friends." "But the train was going down-town not up-town to the Bronx. Why were you in such a rush?" he asked. I didn't answer this. He continued with the questions. "What are you doing in work clothes?" There's something not right here. What's your name and address?" As he was questioning me he pulled out my Drogheda Garda ID—the look on his face was of complete confusion. "Where is this place?" What are you doing in the state of New York?" he asked. I said was on holiday. "Why are you wearing work clothes with a change of clothes in this bag?" he asked. I said I was doing a bit of painting for my girlfriend. "You're coming with me. You're not telling the truth. I don't believe you," replied the cop. I was so afraid. He gave the other officers in the police car a nod and they got out of the car. *I'm in trouble—I'm going down for this* is what I was thinking. It was never my intention to break the law. This was not how my day was meant to end up!

As the cop continued to pull my wallet apart, the NYC PBA World Trade Centre Card that my mate John had given me fell out onto the street and the cop picked it up. He went totally crazy with me shouting at me asking where I got the card. He then started accusing me of stealing the card. "I didn't steal the card," I said. "Shut your mouth you thief! You are going to be spending some time behind bars. I will make sure you get done for this," he shouted at me.

In my head I was asking for help, *please something or somebody help me,* I pleaded. Then I heard the same soft voice in my ear saying, "tell him who gave you the card. I trusted the guidance and said to him

"I got the card from my cousin John. He's a Transit Police Detective."
"Oh did you now? What station does this 'John' guy work from?" he
asked. "He doesn't work from a station he works from an office," I
replied, remembering John had told me to say this if I ever got stopped.
I asked the cop to call John, that he would explain this and confirm
who I was. So the cop rang central station to get diverted to John's
number. I could hear the phone ringing but there was no answer.

He was looking at me and I thought he was starting to twig I was an
illegal! I begged him to call him once more. "Okay one more time," the
cop confirmed. "But if I don't get an answer, you are coming with me."
I heard the phone ringing for one last time. My heart was pounding,
please answer John, I pleaded in my head. I heard John's voice. He
answered the phone. Thank God! The cop started asking John lots of
questions. John confirmed I was his cousin and that he gave me the
NYC PBA card. The cop apologised to me and said "You are lucky
you know John. You do understand why I arrested you?" I apologised
and said I never meant to break the law. With that he removed the
handcuffs from my wrists. I was free!

I thanked him for not arresting me. The cop then asked if he could
help me in any way. "I'm very late now," I said. "Let me put you back
onto the train," he volunteered. I finally made my way to work. What
a morning! I was so relieved to be on the train again! I felt so alive
and grateful to the world. The Universe wanted me to wake up, it was
knocking trying to point me in the right direction, but I had a few more
lessons to learn ...

When I arrived at work I couldn't get through the security. I was
on the street looking up at the roof trying to catch one of the boys'
attention. I saw my boss in his pickup truck pulling up beside me. He
got out and started shouting at me "What the hell happened to you?
The boys rang me to tell me you didn't show up so I had to come into
the city. You are lucky if I don't fire you." I tried to explain to him but
he didn't want to know and for the first time in my life I didn't really
care. I felt so free inside. I didn't care that he would not understand.
He handed me a bag with facemasks I'd asked for the previous night. I
spent the rest of that day counting my blessings and although I didn't

have the awareness at the time I was completely living in the moment that day!

My drama in Americana wasn't due to end yet. There was more to come ...

8

One Bang on the Head Too Many

It was very hot and humid now in the city as we headed into mid-summer. Kim and myself were getting ready for the 4th of July celebrations—Independence Day. This was my first ever Independence Day celebration so I was super excited. We decided we would go to Kim's beach house for the holiday. We packed up our bags and headed to the New Jersey shore for a few days. Kim had suggested we go early so we could enjoy the beach house before everyone else got there. This was my ideal way to holiday—the sun, sea, sand, and good company. When we arrived Kim sorted the bedrooms so we got the biggest room, which was great! We were ready to party! There was a real buzz about the place. It felt like I had found the perfect place with the perfect girl. I was so happy. We spent the next few days on the beach swimming and sunbathing. The weather was amazing. There were lots of parties happening so it was hard to decide which one to go to! I didn't really mind which party we went to but Kim did like to have things organised and since there was such a big group of us, she wanted to make sure that we were all going to the same party.

(Song—*Other Side* David Gray)

Independence Day

4th of July 2002—the day my life changed forever! It was the day that God would send the Angels to find me. It was what I would later call my true awakening.

It was a beautiful sunny day. Everything was beaming. Everything felt so perfect. We spent our day at the beach chatting about the various different parties that we were considering going to. There was one massive party every year, held by a doctor. Most people thought this would be the best one to go to.

We were all going out for a meal before the party. We went to an Italian restaurant, the craic was great. We were all having a laugh and enjoying ourselves. I was meeting a lot of Kim's friends for the first time and as I love meeting new people this was easy for me, especially with the good auld Irish gift-of-the-gab! We finished our meal and decided that it was the doctor's house party we would go to. We stopped off on the way to the party at the off-licence to get some beers. Heineken had just brought out the small cans that looked like a keg of beer so I bought them. It is illegal to drink in public in New Jersey so this was another one of my broken rules to add to the list! Nobody seemed to be too bothered—we were all in the party mode!

I looked at my watch as we arrived at the party—it was 9:11 pm. There were people everywhere on the street and taxis were pulling up with more party people arriving. *WOW this is amazing* I thought to myself. We were all very excited and looking forward to a great night. We started to make our way towards this massive beach house. As we entered the front gates of the house we made our way through the crowd towards the right of the building. It was really warm and sweaty. I was wearing a new pair of jeans which were sticking to me. I'd just opened a can of beer and taken a mouthful to cool myself down a bit. We walked up the side of the house and could hear the music getting louder as we got closer. Then we stepped out onto the back of the house where the party was in full swing.

We stood at the right hand corner of the house debating on what to do next. Some of the group wanted to go onto the beach. Kim and I decided to make our way to the back of the house which meant we had to walk under a wooden deck. The deck was roughly 20 by 20 feet and there were a lot people dancing under it. We pushed our way through the crowd, we were very close to the back of the house. I remember looking through a window as we passed by and everyone was dancing in the house, it felt like I was looking at two different worlds. There was also a crowd of people on top of the deck partying. I was really in the moment soaked up with atmosphere and music! I was walking behind Kim holding her hand as we pushed our way through the crowd. The beats were pumping from the speakers. I remember thinking to myself *I feel so tall*. Everyone was dancing to the music and Kim turned around to me and said "I love this song." The words were no sooner out of Kim's mouth when I heard a loud crack followed by an unmerciful bang on my head. I was knocked unconscious. I was gone. I was surrounded by beautiful calming white light. I knew I wasn't in my body. I started to come back, slowly, my senses were being awakened again. I couldn't see anything. It was total darkness. The first thing that I heard was people screaming, crying for help. "Help me I'm trapped," echoed loudly. I was confused and didn't know what had just happened.

My hearing was affected—it sounded like I was stuck in a tunnel. One minute the voices sounded close up and the next minute they sounded far away. This created even more confusion for me as I struggled to understand what had just happened.

I was pinned to the ground lying face down. Kim's legs were slightly under me. I tried to check to see if Kim was okay. I reached over and put my hand on her back to see if she was breathing. I could feel Kim breathing. At least she was alive. I told her not to move that everything was going to be okay. People were still screaming, crying and shouting for help. All of a sudden I felt so calm which was a surreal moment in the middle of the mayhem. I wasn't to know at this point that it would be the moment of my true awakening. This would be the beginning of my spiritual journey and the Angels fully entering my life.

I couldn't take a full breath. Everything was still in darkness. I was breathing in lots of dust. I heard people moving things, it felt like there was things being lifted. I could hear people saying "lift, lift." I prayed to God that Kim and I would be okay. Then I saw light coming through a gap that the people had cleared. I remember my eyes trying to adjust to the bright light. The gap was just big enough for one person to fit through, so I pulled Kim back and pushed her out through the gap. I then followed, feeling my way out through the gap and as I did I found a pair of ladies shoes. I picked them up and took them with me. I was in deep shock and injured.

My eyes were still adjusting to the light when I got out. There were lots of people lying on the ground. Everyone was in a state of panic. Floodlights lit up the ground where people were being treated by the emergency services. There were people coming over to me asking if I was okay.

"Yes," I replied, "I'm fine, but what exactly happened?" I asked. People weren't exactly sure what happened. From what I could make out, the deck gave way and collapsed coming down on top of us. There were thirty three people trapped and injured. There were no fatalities, we were blessed.

I couldn't feel any pain as I walked around dazed and confused. Amazingly the two cans of beer in my pockets survived the accident, but they were causing me great discomfort. I tried to get them out of my pockets, but it wasn't an easy task as they were wedged in there. Eventually I got them both free.

I was wandering around with the pair of ladies shoes asking if anyone had lost their shoes. I was interrupted by one of Kim's best friends who came over to see if I was okay. "Kim is over there, you need to go the hospital," he suggested. I thought I was okay but he could clearly see the full extent of my injuries. I ignored Kim's friend's advice as I was too preoccupied with my irrational thoughts of being illegal. *What if I got caught?* I was in a state of complete and utter fear.

What if they find out that I've out-stayed my visa? If they arrest me I will be sent straight to police station and then deported? Oh my God, what about all my stuff at my apartment, my friends, Kim and the life I've made here? I don't want to go home I thought to myself. I heard Kim's friend speaking in the background still. I could see his lips moving but all I could think about was running away. I was looking at the beach planning my escape route. "Listen, I'm not legal here. Please don't say anything. I have to get out of here. If I'm caught I will be deported," I said to Kim's friend. He wasn't too shocked on hearing this revelation. "Don't worry Robbie, you will be fine," he said reassuringly. "No, I really have to go," I insisted. His tone got louder "You have to go hospital, you're injured!" I asked him to meet me a couple of miles down the beach. "What about Kim?" he asked with concern. "Tell her I'll be fine." I wasn't thinking straight; the fear of getting caught was so overwhelming. All I could think about was getting away.

As I made my way towards the beach out of nowhere a cop stepped out in front of me. "Hey, where are you going? You're injured." I was panicking inside thinking *I'm caught now. Oh no I'm caught. What am I going to do?* "What's your name and address? Have you any ID on you?" he asked. I said I had no ID on me even though my Passport was in my back pocket! "What's your name?" he asked again. I didn't want to give him my name so I made up a fake name and address. He wrote down my fake details in his book. He then shouted over to a fireman, "This guy needs to go to the hospital." The fireman walked me over to the stretcher. I looked over my shoulder and saw the possibility of freedom slipping away from me!

I was still holding the pair of ladies shoes in my hand as I sat on the stretcher. I saw Kim so I decided to get up and go over to her. I was telling Kim that I needed to get away, to take my passport and I would get it later. Kim was crying, pleading for me to go to hospital. Because I was in so much shock I didn't realise the extent of Kim's injuries or mine. I started asking random girls "Did you lose your shoes?" I looked at Kim and noticed she was not wearing any shoes. I looked up and all of sudden, for the first time, I saw the full extent of Kim's injuries. Her face was covered in blood. That's when the shock really hit me! I collapsed to the ground. I was in so much pain. Kim's mates helped me to the step. I was really hurt. I went to stand up but I couldn't walk. My foot was badly injured along with my neck and back. I had a massive cut down my back and a graze on my knee. I started to hop towards the beach. I could see people staring at me with a look of horror on their faces. Out of nowhere, the same cop that stopped me before stepped out in front of me!

He asked me why I hadn't gone to hospital. I sensed that he was really starting to get suspicious. He took out his book where he wrote my fake name and address down. "What's your name and address again?" he asked. For the life of me I couldn't remember the name and address I had given him, so I said my real name and my address. He looked at his book "that's not the name and address you gave earlier. Who are you here with?" he asked. "I'm with my girlfriend, she's over there," I replied as I pointed over to Kim. Listen, I've just had a deck collapse on me. I don't know one day of the week from the next, so sorry if I couldn't remember my name or address," I protested. He seemed to accept and understand my reason because he gently brought me over to the stretcher Kim was on. He then fetched one for me. "These guys are in a bad way—get them into the next ambulance," he ordered. Then he moved over to Kim's stretcher. They were talking but I couldn't hear what they were saying. I was trying my best to get Kim's attention to make sure she wouldn't tell him I was illegal. When I heard him saying he was coming with us to the hospital I automatically assumed I was going to be arrested, but thankfully the cop got called to something else. I breathed a sigh of relief as we got wheeled into the back of the ambulance. The doors shut. I was safe.

Kim was really worried about getting to hospital. I had no medical insurance. In America if you don't have medical insurance you won't get the full treatment. Kim told me to say I was covered on her policy. I reassured her that everything would be okay. When we arrived at A&E we each got taken to different parts of the emergency room. The doctor sent me for some x-rays and a scan. When the nurse asked me for my insurance details I gave her Kim's policy. The nurse then confirmed what we already knew—I wasn't covered. Therefore I didn't receive full treatment.

The nurses were getting great fun out my Irish accent. It felt like I was the first Irish person they had ever met. To pass the time I watched the TV in my room. One of the nurses came in all excited, telling me I was famous! Our accident was headline news on the local news channel.

We spent about six to eight hours in hospital. They bandaged me up, gave me some painkillers and discharged me. What a way to spend the 4th of July!

The Road to Recovery

Kim's parents took us to their home by the lake to recover. I was in a bad way. My whole body felt broken, but more than this my Spirit was broken. I could have been killed in the accident. Was this all part of God's big plan for me?

This was not the first time in my life where my body had been broken and I felt pain but it was the first time my spirit had been broken. Although I would later call this my true awakening it was the beginning of a slippery slope to a very dark point in my life. As much as I was grateful for being at Kim's parents and their kindness I found it difficult to accept this help. My pride got in the way. I would later find out after I met my Guardian angel that pride had another name—it was the ego mind.

Over the next few days whilst recovering, the pain was still really intense. Although Kim's injuries were bad she was mobile. I couldn't move and spent most days in bed. I had a lot of time to think. My thoughts went deep within. I thought a lot about my family, who at this point were unaware I was in an accident. After a few days I decided to phone home and tell them. They didn't realise how bad the accident was because I put on a brave face saying everything was ok, not wanting to worry them.

Kim's parents were encouraging us to ring a lawyer for compensation. I hadn't told them I was illegal at this point. It was hard for me to lie to them because I had so much respect for them. Kim wasn't telling the truth to her parents either. I really thought if they knew I over-stayed my Visa they would not accept me. Being accepted or the feeling of rejection had deep-rooted issues for me, but now was not the time for me to have full understanding of this part of my life.

As the week passed, I could start to get about a little more but it was still a great struggle. Kim decided to go back to work but I was still not well enough to go back to my apartment in the Bronx. We all sat down for our dinner one evening and the conversation came up again about seeing a lawyer. "I will wait until I get back to the Bronx and then ring," I told them. Kim's dad said "Here's a number a friend gave me. Give him a ring." I went really red in the face with embarrassment. Both her parents disclosed to me at this point "We know Robbie, it's okay. We have known for a while that you're not legal, don't worry."

Whilst Kim was working I stayed with her parents at the lake. I soon decided that I was well enough to go back to my apartment. My sister had been planning a holiday all year to visit me and I didn't want to let her down. Kim tried to persuade me to stay a bit longer. She felt I wasn't well enough to go back to living on my own. I thought I was fine or at least pretending to be fine. I reassured Kim that my friend Neala would be at my place. What I didn't disclose was that Neala was due to go home to Ireland for a trip within the next week or so. I felt I had to stand on my own two feet again. So Kim and I made our way back to the city, and from there I went back to my apartment in the Bronx.

I kept thinking about what Kim's father had said to me about legal advice. I phoned Kim to discuss. Kim felt I should seek advice. So I decided to go to the local Irish centre and ask for advice. I confided with the lady in the centre who gave me the name of an Irish lawyer. I called him to discuss my case. He felt I had a strong case for compensation but was unsure about how my legal status would affect my case. The lawyer set me up with a specialist doctor in the city and I finally started to get some proper medical treatment.

I would travel into the city every day to receive my treatments. As I wasn't working my money was slowly running out. Even paying for the subway into the city most days was starting to get difficult. I began to feel so trapped but my pride wouldn't allow me to ask for help. So I didn't eat as much and didn't buy the painkillers I was being prescribed. I was on a slippery slope.

Making my way around was challenging and the heat didn't help. I hobbled about in my neck collar, back brace and crutches. The one positive thing I had to look forward to was my sister coming to visit. She would be with me for my birthday. I was delighted. I wanted her to have the best time ever!

I decided to save the little money that I had for my sister's trip. I literally lived on bread and water for a week until my sister arrived. That was the toughest week ever. My thoughts were starting to get darker. I was trying hard to block them. It felt like I was in a real battle looking for some glimmer of light at the end of the dark tunnel.

9

Putting on a Brave Face

I was so excited. My sister Vicky and her boyfriend were arriving for a holiday. Even though I was still in a lot of pain, I wanted to show her I was living the dream. I called my mom to make sure Vicky got her flight ok. I had arranged to meet my sister in a bar in the city. I thought that it would be easier to meet there rather than the longer journey to the Bronx. Plus I thought Manhattan would be a nice way for them to start their holiday.

I made me way to the bar, hanging around waiting for them to arrive. I asked the bar person to check the flights on teletext. She confirmed the flight from Dublin had landed on schedule. I enjoyed a beer whilst waiting for them to arrive. An hour passed and there was no sign of my sister and her boyfriend. I asked the bar person to double check if the right flight had landed. The flight had definitely landed she confirmed. I called my mom again to make sure they had gotten the flight. Mom assured me they had got the flight. They were now an hour and a half late. I was starting to worry, so I decided to have a look out on the street. Which way do I go—left or right? A strong sense came over me that I needed to go left. I trusted my gut and went left. I walked until the end of the block. Again, having to make a choice—left or right? As I stood at the corner of this block looking onto an avenue, I felt a strong urge to go right. I walked for about 5 minutes across about eight blocks and I decided to stop. I thought to myself, *how am I going to find my sister in the middle of New York?*

I was getting concerned at this point. I was considering turning back when I heard a familiar voice. I looked across the street and in the distance I saw my sister's long blonde hair. I smiled to myself, *thank God they have arrived.*

I started whistling as loud as I could and waving my hands in the air. She turned around and waved back and started making her way towards me.

I asked her what had happened. They gave the taxi driver the address for the bar and he drove around for ages in circles saying he couldn't find the bar. The taxi driver got frustrated and dumped them both at this corner. After being dumped by the taxi driver, Vicky had been standing on the side of the street crying thinking she would not get to see me, spending the whole trip to New York in a hotel! It was so good to see her. It took the whole focus off my accident and injuries. My sister being my sister wanted to know all the details. She was also excited to meet Kim.

Vicky's holiday had officially started. I was so happy. We were all back in the bar. The craic was great. The beer was flowing. My sister couldn't believe that I knew so many people. Nearly every person that walked through the doors of the bar said hello to me by my name. She was having a good auld laugh saying it was just like I was back home in Drogheda! Before we knew it the clock said 9 pm. We were having such a good time we didn't feel the hours pass by. We were all a little tipsy at this stage so I asked my sister if she would like to get a taxi home, which took about 50 minutes. Or we could take the subway and she could see Harlem, the Yankee Stadium and how beautiful the city looked by night. She looked to me and said "whichever you think is best Robbie. You know the city better than we do!" I suggested the subway. It takes a bit longer, but it throws you right into the middle of the Manhattan madness. Famous last words ...

It Was Like the Movie Scene From "Ghost"

I gave my sister the do's and don'ts of travelling on the subway. "If you make any eye contact, don't stare, look away. When we get down onto the platform make sure you stand back from the edge of the line," I advised.

My sister had enough suitcases to last for two months! "What did you pack Vicky, your entire wardrobe? She laughed and said "that's to carry some extra clothes on the way home. This is bargain City!" I laughed to myself thinking, *with all these bags she must be planning to bring all 5th avenue home with her, typical Irish.*

We were getting close to subway station. My sister was looking up at the height of all the buildings. I joked with her saying "if the wind changes you will end up stuck that way." When we arrived at the station I saw my sister was a little apprehensive. I reassured her that we would be fine and I continued to crack the jokes.

Our train arrived in. We found a seat for the three of us together right inside the door, the closest seat to the adjoining carriage. I was on the right hand-side, Vickie was in the middle and her boyfriend was on the left. It had been a really hot day so you can imagine the humidity on the subway. To make matters worse you couldn't feel the air-con until the train pulled off. The doors of the subway carriage closed (Bing Bong) and the train started to pick up speed.

Next thing the door slid open from the adjoining carriage. A big black guy about 6ft tall wearing a trench coat buttoned right up to the neck slammed the carriage door closed. I wasn't really paying too much attention to him as I was daydreaming. He took a couple of steps and suddenly stopped facing my sister. Out of nowhere he started screaming at her "HEY YOU WHITE SLUT! YOU FUCKING WHITE SLUTS! YOU LOVE DILDOS!" This all happened so fast. I was trying to register what was going on. I looked over to my sister's boyfriend—he had lost all colour in his face with this look like he was frozen in his seat. My sister was glued to her seat. I was thinking *what the hell is going on here? As* this man is screaming in her face. My sister was wearing a v neck t-shirt and a chain with a crucifix, it was real bling! It was an eye catcher. Things were going in slow motion. He was still shouting at my sister "Who do think you are? White bitch wearing that cross—do you know Jesus is black?" I quickly remembered my uncle telling us a story when we were kids about being nearly mugged on a train. He got up and started to act like he was crazy. Just like clockwork I began to sense the presence around us and I heard the voice in my head saying *get up do something, your sister needs your help.* I got up and started screaming and barking like I was a dog! I was slapping myself on the face and acting really crazy. I started screaming "Come on, I will take you, pick on me." I'm making all these funny noises whilst banging my hands on my chest. Well, let me tell you this guy didn't know what hit him. He had met his match! He must have gotten some fright because the next thing he's running down the carriage. I was shouting at him "Come back here. I will sort you." When I turned around my sister was having a massive panic attack. Her boyfriend looked like he had just seen a ghost. I asked Vicky if she was okay. Everyone on the train started clapping. They all looked happy that I had stood up to this guy. I was just happy that we were all safe. I had to stay strong for my sister but let me tell you, my knees where knocking. I spent the rest of the train ride home saying to my sister that this was a 'one off'.

'East 235th Street Next Stop'

When we arrived in the Bronx, I was really thinking about the events that were happening and questioning them in my mind. It's funny how we mask things but inside we are screaming and I was starting to break down, but I couldn't name it or even describe what I felt inside. I was beginning to feel so separate from everything and I was losing my faith, but I can't say why. This darkness was around me, it was the beginning of a major turning point in my life. We arrived at my apartment. I had only one air-con unit and the heat was unbearable, so I set it up in my room and my sister and her boyfriend stayed there. I was used to the heat at night so I didn't mind, but I felt for my sister. It must have been some shock to the system and what an eventful day!

We spent the next few days travelling around the city, I was having great fun and showing Vicky all the sites. The empire state building was amazing. I had a friend of a friend who worked in the elevators fixing them, so we didn't have to get a ticket or queue. Vicky and her boyfriend felt like VIPs, in fact we all did, this was such a special moment for me. I was defiantly the best tour guide as we visited the different sites. I hadn't much cash but I kept a brave face on because I was always conscious of not letting Vicky down. However, I knew somewhere deep inside she could see me struggle. We floated around the city from the Intrepid Warship Museum to Central Park. Vicky really wanted to see ground Zero. I hadn't been down there in quite a while, Vicky was so eager to cross the walking bridge and get some photos. We went down one morning and of course Vicky was asking lots of question, most of which I couldn't answer. I told her that she would see for herself. There were lots of people visiting and paying their respects and my heightened sensitivity to things didn't help me. When we arrived at ground zero I could see the shock on Vicky's face. She looked up to the sky all around her and tried to imagine how tall the buildings really were and the sheer terror there was that day. Vicky told me that on 9/11 mom and dad and all the family were so worried about me. Vicky said "I now understand what you experienced." It was all so life changing and my journey was still very much at the beginning and the day of reckoning was soon to come.

10

Living it up in the Big Apple

(Song—*Empire state of mind* Jay/z, Alica keys)

My birthday was coming up and I wanted to celebrate whilst Vicky was over. Kim had arranged for us to go to this amazing restaurant. Kim was so kind and thoughtful, always thinking and doing for others. We all got dressed up and hit the big bright lights of the city, everyone was super excited. We arrived at this amazing restaurant and it was so special, the food was great and the atmosphere felt electric. Kim had really spoiled me and it was so great to be in that special moment with the people I really loved. When we left the restaurant Kim had arranged a limousine for us to go down town to Greenwich Village and we ended up in a bar called the Red Lion. The drinks were flowing and we were singing and dancing the night away. The village is really an amazing place with lots of body piercing and tattoo shops. Someone decided that we should all get something done to mark the occasion. This sounded like a great idea at the time and being Irish we were always up for a laugh and a bit of craic. So we left the pub and we staggered around looking into shop windows. We finally found a tattoo shop that looked really good. The next moment we were inside debating on whether to get a tattoo or a piercing. Vicky, being the most sober was recording all this on camcorder. Thinking this was all so funny we decided to get a piercing and then we had to choose one for each other. Let me tell you that wasn't a good idea. I decided that Vicky's boyfriend was to have his lip pierced, it looked really painful. Next it was Kim's turn and we picked the top part of her ear to be pierced and all Kim could think about was what her parents and people at work would say about it. Kim screamed the whole time during the piercing. We were all laughing thinking *this is such a great idea*. Then it was my turn and they decided that I would get the inside of my earlobe pierced, well did that hurt! And all we heard was an American girl screaming "OH MY GOD you guys are crazy!" Vicky was the only sensible one but made sure to get some good video evidence. We all left the tattoo parlour and rode the limo up town. I asked the driver to open the sunroof so we could stand up, look out and scream our heads off just like the movie scene in 'BIG,' this was the best night ever. We were all pretty smashed so it was back to Kim's and bedtime.

Sore Heads and an Ears

We awoke the next morning and I had a really sore head. As I lifted my head from the pillow I could feel my ear. It was so sore and just for a brief moment I couldn't remember getting my ear pierced. Kim was the same. We looked at each other and couldn't believe it. We both had really sore heads but to top it off our ears were sore too. I got up and woke Vicky up and we sat in Kim's apartment that morning. All Kim could think about was work and her parents, but it was all fun at the time. We had the weirdest breakfast ever that morning. I had been telling Vicky about this Mexican restaurant that we ordered from all the time and it didn't matter what time you order, day or night, they were opened and delivered. So it was burritos and salad bowls for breakfast. I know it doesn't sound nice but in that moment I was so happy. All the thoughts and pain were gone and I was just loving having my sister to visit.

11

The Dark Soul of the Night

(Song—*Hurt* Johnny Cash)

In the back of my mind I knew how much Vicky was helping me while she was over and I was starting to feel guilty that they were using some of their holiday money on me. This was where I started to really turn from my light and it's when the dark soul of the night started to creep in. At this point I felt like I had nothing and it was so hard not to listen to the voice in 'my head' as it talked to me. I tried to block it out but I could start to feel it slowly taking a hold of my positive thoughts and replacing them with thoughts of no self-worth. I was hiding this from Kim and especially Vicky, as she too was so sensitive and would notice that there was something wrong. *Why could I not ask for help?* At this time I was so lost, I realise now that I was suffering from post-traumatic stress. All I knew was that the accident that could have killed me might as well have because I was now facing this person. I didn't know who I was and I hadn't got the coping mechanism to move forward, the walls were closing in. If I kept smiling no one would see through me. I was so afraid that people might see my pain. I was so hard on myself and not wanting to fail and this really made me more determined not to break down and ask Kim or Vicky for help. This was part of my lesson I would find out later and it would teach me the most valuable lesson in my life.

Only Through My Darkness Could I Find My Light!

The morning I was dreading had arrived, Vicky was going home to Ireland. As she packed up her things we were chatting and she said to me "why don't you come home Robert? There is no shame. We all think you have done well. Things are too hard for you here and with your injuries you can't work, what are you going to do for work and money?" she asked "I will find something" I replied. I felt I had no life back in Ireland and if I went back I would probably start walking in my old shoes. I wanted to stay away from that part of my old life style. I knew there and then that I should have said yes but the words just wouldn't come. I had too much pride and Oh my god, but can it prohibit you from making the right choice. Vicky cried "We all love you please come back home, please come home". We were both crying it hurt so bad as I looked at Vicky, but I couldn't make the choice, it was like Vicky knew what was happening but didn't know how to help. She gave me the last of her holiday money and said to me "you will need this more than me." I had such a lump in my throat. The taxi was on its way and my feelings and emotions were all over the place. I was trying to be strong so I wouldn't worry Vicky and didn't want to worry my family.

The Taxi had arrived and it was time to say goodbye. I said to Vicky "will you tell everyone at home I love them so much?" We were bringing the luggage to the taxi and Vicky is asking If I will be okay I replied "I will be fine don't you be worrying. I will call down to see Kim later." I said this doing the big brother thing and I also didn't want to send any smoke signals home that there might have been something wrong. We were saying our goodbyes. Vicky got into the taxi and I had only a minute or two before they left. I was saying goodbye but in my head what I am really saying is *please take me home* and Vicky said to me again "come home, you won't be a failure."

I closed the door of the taxi and stepped back onto the sidewalk and as the taxi started pulling away I looked into my sisters eyes thinking *please don't go*! I looked again right into hers eyes for that one last time and something snapped inside me and I thought that it would be the last time I would see her. The Dark Soul of night had its grip on me. The taxi turned the corner and they were gone and I had never felt so alone in my life. That day I felt so separate and as I looked out into the world all I could feel was my darkness. *Why did I just not go home?* I went back into the apartment crying, like a lost sheep looking for its shepherd. The dark soul of the night would present itself this day. Its voice became no longer within my mind and as it spoke to me it started beating me down saying 'you are not strong, you're a failure, you're worthless, you are not loved'. Can you imagine what I was going through? I had no answers for this, it was like a black cloud had come over me, I could see no light, only my darkness. I had no understanding of love at this point, no understanding of forgiveness. I was thinking of ending my life. I felt worthless and the Dark Soul made sure it suppressed and diminished any light that I had. I had hit an all-time low and I just couldn't see my way out. I always say at this point in my life, all I had left in my Soul as it cried out for help was one particle of light, the rest was surrounded by darkness. I wanted to die that day and those emotions were coming from a place that was so dark within my soul. I hated myself and felt that my life was meaningless. I hadn't got the strength to get away from this as it called to me 'take your own life, you are unloved, you have failed.'

I was in my bedroom still crying. I had a little notice board and on this I had a painting my mother gave me before I left for America. It was a painting of Christ's hands with some rosary beads around them. It meant so much to me but because I was so disconnected at this point I couldn't see its true value. I remember my mother saying that this would protect me and watch over me. I was looking at the painting but felt no connection, it was like something crept in and took it all from me. I was angry. I was thinking of my brothers, Joe and Jason, my sister Vicky, my mom and dad as I was starting to contemplate taking my life. My aim was to do this so I wouldn't hurt any more. So I could be free of all the things that were in my head, never once thinking that I was loved. I wasn't doing this to hurt anyone.

I also had my uncle and aunt's phone number on this board. They lived in Boston. My mom gave me their number and said if I ever needed them just call. I went to bed early that night feeling very depressed. I cried myself to sleep. I spent the next day or two in a very dark place. Kim called asking why I didn't get in touch. I lied and said that I was busy. Kim asked if I was okay that I didn't sound like I was in a good place. I smoothed it over saying I was just sad that Vicky had gone and just felt a bit lonely. Kim invited me to come and stay with her in the city for a couple of days. I told her I would come over and stay at the weekend. Poor Kim had no idea I was in so much pain, that I hurt and to top it off, I felt so guilty lying to her saying I was fine. This was so out of character for me. I was always such a straight guy. Kim told me she loved me and I said "I will see you later."

There will never be a single soul that the love of God will not instil Hope, as God beckons us towards the light, at every single moment in darkness & light. Every soul carries the light of God Within them.

Time to See If My Time Was Up Here?

I made the decision to end my life and this was so mental on many levels. How did I end up at this point? I came to America to create the perfect life, to prove to myself that I could make a difference and be the person I felt was somewhere deep inside. To get away from all the hurt and pain of my childhood to which I had no answers. This is the land where your dreams can come true, the land of opportunity, but mine were so far removed from that reality. I took the money Vicky gave me and I went to the local deli where I bought drink and lots of tablets. The guy behind the counter knew me from coming into the deli all the time. He did give me a look like *what hell was I doing*? But he never said anything. I was so focused at this point. I had tunnel vision and the tunnel I was looking down had no light at the end of it. I went back to the apartment and started to drink and as I spent the day drinking, I took all my photos I had with me and started looking through them. I was in a battle with myself. My will to die was so strong it dampened out the sounds of not going through with it. I got a pen and paper and started to write a final letter to my family telling them how sorry I was and how much I loved them. Writing was never my best skill. I am left-handed and in school this was nearly beaten out of me. As I wrote the first letter I started making some spelling mistakes, so I crumpled that one up and a few more after that. My soul would cry out that night and it would be heard in the heavens. I was drinking and getting drunk which made everything seem more heightened. It amplified everything for me. I was getting close to taking the tablets so I opened the bottle of spirits as I was finishing my letter. How sad was I? How did my life end up here? I was so angry with God. I had no faith. Why does there have to be so much pain in this world? Everywhere I look I see people struggling and suffering. I was totally in my free will at that moment, choosing to end it all. Even though I was blaming the world because my understanding at that time had no other meaning, there was no turning back.

I opened the tablets and took them one at a time, drinking to wash them down. I started to fold up all my stuff on the bed. In the middle of my madness whilst the tears were dripping down my face, I thought to myself *what am I doing?* But the Dark Soul was with me. I was starting to feel the effects and I was shouting out "sorry mom and dad, please forgive me". The pain I was feeling at this point was unreal, even to this day I can't describe it and I will never find the words to express it. I had the phone in my room so I went and put the phone into the holder in the living room and staggered back to my room and locked the door. I was starting to feel weak and slipping in and out of consciousness as I finished the last of the tablets. My life was starting to flash in front of me. I was seeing different memoires of my life. I was delirious with so much drink and tablets, *what have I done?* I looked at my board and my mom's picture, and for that moment I can remember my last thoughts as I called out

PLEASE SAVE ME, PLEASE FORGIVE ME, FOR I KNOW NOT WHAT I DO

Divine Intervention

(Song—*Tear Drop* Massive Attack)

I came around as I was lying on the floor and I heard a voice. The phone was in my hand and it was my Aunt Tammy and Uncle Brian on the other end saying "hang in there we love you." I was still slipping in and out of consciousness and they kept me on the phone talking. My room was full of light, it was like the sun it was so bright but it was the middle of the night. I hadn't a clue how the phone had gotten into my hand? How did I ring Brian and Tammy. I felt so sick and I was still pretty out of it. I looked over to my board and my mother's painting was gone. I was so confused. I was talking to Brian and he was really worried! I wasn't making much sense. I asked "How did you ring me?" He replied "I didn't, the phone rang and it was you on the other end. Are you okay? Hang in there I will come for you." They stayed on the phone for a good while until I was making more sense. Oh I felt like crap! *What have I done? I tried to kill myself and I survived. I can't even do that right! I'm a total failure.* I still couldn't understand how the phone got into my room. As I became more aware the brightness in the room started to recede. The feeling in the room was so strong, it was the same presence I had felt as a child and other events leading up to this moment but it was a million times stronger. I was looking around the room for my mom's picture but I couldn't see it and I was thinking to myself *I put four pins in it so it wouldn't come off the board, where could it be?* I went to my bedroom door and it was still locked. I opened the door and went towards the living room to get some water. I was very badly dehydrated and I passed the phone holder and there was my mom's painting right next to the holder. I couldn't believe it. *What the hell is going on?*

I survived somehow and for me this was the next major part of my awakening. Brian was on his way to me from Boston. I was in such a dark place but really grateful to be alive. I was feeling very guilty and I wasn't sure how Brian would react when he arrived. As I waited for Brian to arrive I couldn't stop thinking about how mom's picture ended up in the living room and how the phone ended up in my room? The time was coming where I would be asking the biggest question of my whole life and all the things I had sensed as a child, young adult and now in my early twenties. Yet I was still very much in denial. So I had a little bit more to go. Things were going to change from this day and it was never going to be same. From this moment my life would start and my soul's purpose and true journey would begin.

Brian arrived the next morning. He was someone I always looked up to, a very wise soul. I put on a brave face but there was no doubt he could see straight through this and he never once said anything. He showed nothing but unconditional love and understanding to me and asked me to come back to Boston with him. I had no intention of doing this but he convinced me to come and stay for a few weeks 'until you feel better'.

All I could think about was Kim; Brian said "Give her a call and let her know that you're staying with us." I phoned Kim and told her I was going to stay in Boston for a few weeks. Kim didn't know the reason I was going and was a little pissed off with me. I never told her what had happened, that I had tried to take my own life. As I spoke to Kim on the phone I felt so sad, it was like a major shift, a disconnection had happened. I could feel her move from my heart. I felt like I had let her down so badly after everything she had helped me with. I was remembering all the good and happy times and the love Kim had for me. But I still didn't know how to love myself, I was broken and trying to find the man I was within. As I packed my stuff for my journey to Boston, Brian was so kind compassionate and understanding, he was just shining so much light on me. Leaving New York I was thinking the whole time *I will be back, I'm only going to stay up with Brian and Tammy for a few weeks until I feel better.* Little did I know!

(Song—*Kathy* Eva Cassidy)

12

The Awakening
(The Light of God Will Always Find You)

Our journey was going to take five hours and I worried about what we would talk about during this time. I hoped he wouldn't ask me too much about what I just tried and why. On our way we spoke about many things, about my mom and about my childhood. We also spoke about God and spirituality. I totally closed down and I went into judgement mode. I let the voice of everyone else's dogma wash over me, they were bible bashers. All I was thinking was that they weren't going to convert me. I'm just staying a couple of weeks and getting the hell out of 'Dodge City' and back to New York. This may sound ungrateful but it was just where I was at this time. What my journey would soon reveal to me was that they were both very spiritual people with great understanding and wisdom but my immaturity couldn't see through this at that time. I am sure we all have done this before, listened to someone else's view and created a judgment based on that view. I was starting to learn a little about love, compassion and forgiveness, but in a really subtle way as Brian kept shining his light.

We arrived in Boston and it was great to see Tammy and the kids, they gave me a really warm welcome and had a room ready for me in the basement. I was so happy to be with family but they were different to any one I had ever been with before and trying to find the words would do it no justice. They were just so in tune with the world, the universe, God and life. I had only arrived and I could already sense this. It was very different to my family home, this house was very relaxed and had such loving vibes.

I spent my first week sleeping. I had a black depression so I found it hard to get motivated. Brian and Tammy were so supportive. I felt so safe but still had a lot of stuff going on in my mind, plus I was beginning to experience paranormal activity and this was a really confusing time for me. This seemed to happen more around me when I was in my room and I thought I was losing my mind. I didn't know what to say to Brian and Tammy even though I knew they would totally understand. My belongings were being moved in my bedroom, then they would go missing and turn up exactly where I had left them. I was starting to see stuff moving around my room. I'd light a candle and it would elevate across the room. I was starting to wonder if I was going crazy! I thought if I said anything to Brian and Tammy I would end up in a psychiatric ward and after trying to take my own life, it would have made a strong case so I kept it zipped.

In the evening time I would come and eat with the family. Brian began to speak to me about how he found it hard to cope after his father died. He explained that he went to see a man who could communicate with the dead. I really trusted him, if this was anyone else saying this to me I would have closed down. Hearing this from Brian I knew he would not tell a lie. He had a way of making me feel at ease, never pushing me into their beliefs. I didn't tell them I was experiencing all this crazy stuff like the bedside lamp going on or off after I plugged it out. I was still trying to cope with my life and past and as we spoke he had this amazing ability to get into my past and talk about it.

This was something I had never done in my life up to this point. We didn't speak about problems at home growing up. This was all new to me. I found this really hard but as I say I really trusted him and this did make my life a lot easier. I was in the cave as I spent the week sleeping and resting. I did start to come out of my cave but for the first time in my whole life I was facing Robbie. I was trying to understand how complex I was as a person and talking about things I had buried inside me for most of my life and had never spoken about. My childhood would come up a lot but I was not ready to face my demons. For me the process was one step at a time. My wounds where deep, however the love I was shown was something I will always be grateful for.

Tammy's grandmother had a swimming pool so we would go there most evenings and barbeque and swim. This helped me with my injuries and recovery and it was great to spend time with Tammy's family. Her grandmother was the most straight talking lady I have ever met and had a sense humour like I had never witnessed. There was lots of laughter and laughter is definitely good soul therapy. I was thinking of home and my mom. I was feeling home sick but it wasn't that I wanted to live at home. Funny, I know I just worried about my mom because I knew she was finding it hard to cope as she was still mourning my grandfather.

I phoned home to speak with my family and tell them I was living with Brain and Tammy for a short while. I didn't phone home often as I didn't want to encourage any late night phone calls. This would be a time when my mom would come home from a night out and would be really upset. It's not that I didn't want to speak to her but if I took a late night phone call I would have to listen to all the hurt and pain that she was still stuck in, it was like she couldn't move on. I felt that she was just in such a dark place at the time. I was also in a dark place and I found it hard to cope with myself so I didn't want to clash with mom but it was great to chat.

I hadn't spoken to Kim since I left Manhattan and I had this massive block with that, *what was wrong with me?* I couldn't cope. I was meant to ring Kim but I was putting it off. I was procrastinating and deep down inside I knew I shouldn't do this, however I felt trapped inside my emotions, my whole life had just been turned upside down and it was time to try and find the person I was within. I hadn't the strength to face our relationship. Brian and Tammy introduced me to a friend, he was a painter and they asked him if he would give me a couple of days work. He told them he would have to look at what jobs were coming up but he was unsure because I was illegal.

We received a phone call to the house early one morning. It was Doug the family friend I was introduced to saying he had a few days' work for me. He asked if I would be able to start that morning. "Yes, what time will I be ready for?" I asked. "Now," Doug replied. "What do you mean now?" I asked! "Take a look outside, can you see a white van?" he replied. I looked out of the window, and I saw a white van. "Well that's me" he said! When I think back of this and as I write this, it still makes me laugh that it would be the start of a very interesting relationship. I put the phone down and I rushed to grab some clothes. Tammy packed me some lunch, she was so happy for me.

I went to work that morning with Doug and the sun was shining. He was very laid back, but what I found funny was from the moment I got into the van we connected straight away. The conversation was nice and light. He asked me if I had done any painting before. "Honestly, only a little," I replied. "Well, you have come to the right man! I will teach you how to paint—I have 30 years painting experience. I am going to teach you all I know". Now of course I was delighted and thought this was great. I was getting cash in my hand and working outside in the sun. We arrived at the job and Doug asked me to set him up and put the sheets on the ground so there wouldn't be any paint spills.

I was surprised at the perfectionist in me that appeared on my first day working with Doug. He instructed me to paint a back wall—I spent all morning painting this wall. When Doug appeared to see what I'd done he was shocked at how long it took me—he had painted half the front of the house in the same amount of time!

During our lunch break Doug was asking me lots of questions about my circumstances, like why I was staying with Brian and Tammy and why I was illegal? I was changing the conversation at every given opportunity because I didn't know Doug too well and I didn't feel comfortable sharing my whole life-story with him. What I was hearing from him was that he was on a spiritual journey and had some sort of tragic past. He wasn't giving too much away about himself though.

When I got in that day from work Tammy told me Kim had phoned, she thought I should ring her back and let her know I was okay. I arrived home bright red from the sun and let me tell you the colour wasn't long draining from me. Inside I was saying to myself *Robbie go ring her*, but another other part of me couldn't do it. I didn't know what to say so I told Tammy I would call that evening but I didn't. I felt like crap. I wasn't trying to hurt Kim and I most certainly didn't want to put myself through any more pain. But I was also in the middle of my madness with all the things going on around me. I went to bed that night and it felt as if the universe was highlighting things for me. I didn't sleep well, somewhere in the middle of the night I could hear the answering machine click on. I heard my mother's voice as she left a message, it started off light and friendly and quickly deteriorated into a rant. I was lying in bed and I was feeling sick in the pit of my stomach. I felt really anxious, it was horrible and reminded me of the feelings I had from my childhood. So I had Kim calling that day and my mom calling that night and I couldn't answer either. I woke up the next morning feeling really angry with my mom. "Your mom left a message last night," Brian told me. "I heard her," I replied. He told me it wasn't bad, she was just hurting.

I went to work that day and Doug knew that there was something up with me. I didn't want to speak about my life to him so I masked it off put my head down and painted but for the whole day I was so angry. Doug started to open up to me talking about his life. It sounded very similar to mine when I was on the drink and drugs. He started preaching to me about the do's and don'ts of life. I have to say I was so caught up in my own crap I didn't completely tune in. It was lunchtime and Doug told me he had to go away for an hour and said "If I'm not back just start back to work yourself." Doug was gone a good hour and a half and when he came back he was full of chat and looked a lot lighter. I didn't really ask what was going on but I could see the difference in him. He was a real joker and full of joy and wasn't long getting me to laugh. We would listen to the radio and sing along to the songs. We were like two brothers who knew each other all our lives even though it was only a short while.

For the next couple of days he would disappear at lunchtime. I would take a break by myself. I will never forget the silence as I spent this time alone. I reflected a lot about trying to kill myself in my apartment and also trying to remember back to my childhood, but I couldn't unlock the answers so that frustrated me. I would come home from work each evening and Tammy would say "Kim called again," but I just couldn't pick up the phone and call Kim back and the longer I left it the harder it got. I was a man acting like a child with Tammy making excuses for me and also lying for me. I should have never put her in that position. I didn't have the answers at this time in my life and if I did it would have been a lot easier. It was easier to hide even though I was causing hurt and pain. I finished my first week with Doug and he asked me to work with him the following week. I was happy with that. I spent that weekend chilling with Brian and Tammy and the kids. We went to the beach and the weather was amazing.

On Saturday night as I lay in bed I heard the phone ringing upstairs and at this time of the night, who else could it have been only my mom? I went up the stairs and answered the phone. The conversation started off okay, but as it continued mom started ranting again. I hadn't got much patience. I was like a hot head probably not having enough empathy and compassion for my mom's pain. It felt for me that I had always listened to the same story so I was angry. I asked my mom not to call the house in the middle of the night as it wasn't fair on everyone else in the house, plus the kids were sleeping. My mom went straight into defence-mode, it was like a red rag to a bull. She said it was her brother's home and she would ring whenever she felt like it. I was her son and she would speak to me in whatever way she wanted. We argued for a few moments. I hung up and disconnected the phone. It was all I could do so I wouldn't wake the house up with us fighting. This was a really hard time for me, my whole life was upside down and I felt very hurt and confused. I loved my mom and didn't want to be fighting with her, the anxious feelings were back.

When I got up the next day I knew Brian and Tammy had heard the conversation. Brian was so understanding and reassured me things would be okay. I spent that day in my room feeling so depressed and I had this dread now about the phone ringing, was it going to be mom or Kim? Neither one could I face.

It was Monday morning and I was feeling like crap. This black depression was hanging over me. Doug arrived, I could hear him upstairs. I was down stairs and I didn't want to go to work. Tammy called down a couple of times saying Doug was there. All I wanted to do was get back into bed and feel like crap for the day, but this was not the answer. Tammy came down and asked if I was okay. I told her I didn't want to go in as I felt crap. Well she wasn't buying it. It was time for a bit of tough love. "Well you better go up and tell Doug you won't be going in," she told me. I was half expecting Tammy to do this for me but she said "no you're a man, so act like one".

I went up the stairs and Doug was his usually happy bright self "what's up with you? We're going to be late. Come on get your act together." I was thinking in my head *what will I say?* Before I got a chance to speak Doug said "get your ass out to that van, you started this job with me and by hell will you will finish it. You have two minutes. I will see you at the van."

Tough love, but it motivated me to get ready. Doug started to talk about different things in his life, his relationship with his parents and how he ended up abusing drink and drugs. He had many failed relationships in his life and it took many years to find peace. He asked me lots of questions and I opened up a bit. I told him about different times in my life and he totally understood. I told him about how I tried to kill myself. He had so much compassion! So yet again the universe brought me just what I needed at that moment.

Doug asked me if I wanted to join him for a lunch this one particular day. I asked him where he was going. "I go to a meeting every day. An AA meeting—it's for people with drink problems. There are also people there with drug problems. We meet every day and share our stories. I think it will help you when you hear what other people have been through," Doug suggested. "How will this help me? I asked. "I am not an alcoholic." Admittedly I suppose I was a binge drinker and I did take drugs in the past so I was curious to learn more about this programme. Doug informed me that an alcoholic wasn't necessarily someone who drinks every day and night, which I foolishly believed to be true. Doug explained that an alcoholic could be someone who simply doesn't know how to stop drinking after one drink.

When we arrived at the AA meeting I was shocked at all the different types of people that were there. It wasn't at all like what I had visualised in my head. I wasn't paying too much attention to begin with but when the first person got up to speak I started to tune in. This person talked about all the pain they had in their life and how they had hit rock bottom and from that their life had changed. They also talked about spirituality and God. I wasn't ready to fully accept this, but I was willing to listen. As the meeting continued over lunch, different people would share—men, woman, young and old. At the end I was invited to share my story but I declined. I didn't feel like I had anything to contribute. I was surprised at how much happier and better I felt after this meeting. Although I struggled with the whole God thing!

Doug was like my mentor. He was really helping me. We spent the next few days going to the AA meetings. I was getting a lot from them. When I told Brian and Tammy about Doug and I going to the AA meetings for our lunch they thought it was amazing. I could really feel myself opening up. I started to notice things more when I was painting, like the sounds in nature. It was like my antenna was starting to receive different stations.

What was really being highlighted for me at these meetings was the argument my mom and I had. I didn't want the disharmony to continue with my mom. I confided in Doug about my feelings. "It's funny Robbie, but God will always give to you a moment to heal at any point. All you have to do is listen," he told me. This went in one ear and out the other. I felt I was separate from God and didn't even know if God was real.

Doug suggested I speak at the next meeting. With Doug's support I stood up and spoke for ten minutes. I still don't remember what I said but it felt great! Like the weight of the world had been lifted off my shoulders. My thoughts were of my mom and how much I loved her in that moment. It was a moment of bliss. When we returned to work that day, I felt like I was floating because I had let go of some of the anger I was holding onto.

What happened next was one of my first experiences of synchronicity. I was up on the ladder painting away with the radio playing in the background. We were listening to a country station. I was thinking about my mom, saying sorry in my head to her. Next thing I heard the DJ on the radio announcing a song by an Irish pop band called Boy-Zone. They were my mom's favourite band. *Freaky* I thought! Boy-Zone was never played on this radio station. Then the DJ announced the song he was going to play which was my mom's favourite—

(Song—*No Matter What* Boyzone)

I nearly fell off the ladder! I screamed at Doug "Do you hear this song?" Doug looked at me like I was losing the plot! I couldn't believe my mom's favourite song was being played on the radio. Was this the Universe saying hello or what? When things like this happen, and they are happening all the time, we really need to be aware of the messages we a receiving. They are always trying to help us. It is our job to tune in and listen. This would be my last week working with Doug as he had no more cash jobs. My time with Doug was invaluable. This was a very important part of my journey.

13

Light and Shadows

I had started to see shadows and different colours around people. I thought I was going crazy. I was living with lots of fear. I would go to bed at night and sometimes the shadows would appear, some of which didn't feel nice—they would make the hairs stand on the back of your neck! The room would get so cold. I would close my door because when I looked out into the rest of the basement I could see where the dark shadows were coming in, it was really weird.

I would hide my head under the blankets and pray that they would go away, it worked for sure. It's funny, I was an adult and for the first time in my life I was sleeping with light on and hiding under the blankets!

The shadows were like a silhouette, an outline that resembled a human body but not all of these shadows would make the hair stand on the back of the neck. It was like they had different energies. I was also seeing round balls of light and colours. The balls of light would dance around my room at night. The colours I was seeing were beautiful and vibrant. I would later find out that this was my Angels and Spirit Guides. I then started to see flashes of light around people, like sparkles. *What is going on?* I asked myself.

Brian and Tammy had all these amazing spiritual books. We had great discussions every evening about life and our purpose in life. They were interesting and had great depth. Tammy suggested I should read one of the books because she felt it would help me. I hadn't confided in Tammy or Brian about my experiences, yet they somehow just knew! They were like my spiritual parents, helping me, guiding me and pointing me towards my path. I still had lots of resistance and questions. I had never read a book in my life up until this point. It wasn't something I thought I could do because of my negative school experiences. Tammy continued to insist I read this one particular book. "I have the perfect book for you Robbie," she would say. To get her off my back I took the book and threw it on the floor of my bedroom with no interest whatsoever!

Two steps forward, three steps back.

The Demon Drink Shows Its Face Again

I had made some new friends in the area. Tammy and Brian knew their parents and had told me that as much as these guys were nice they sometimes could get into a bit of trouble. "Don't be trying to drink with these guys," Tammy warned. I didn't really listen to her advice but I would soon learn a lesson very quickly!

We went out on a one-day pub-crawl, playing pool and drinking beers. It was fun and we were having a good time until we got to this one bar. I was feeling tipsy and in hindsight should have called it a day, but one of the guys started drinking whiskey and asked me to have a shot of it with him. When I said no the slagging and piss taking started so I gave in to the peer pressure and began throwing back the shots of whiskey! It started to become a competition to see who could drink the most! "I thought you Irish could drink," he teased. Half-a-bottle of whiskey later I wasn't making much sense.

A guy at the bar asked if we wanted to play a game pool for money. We had been holding the pool table for a good few games at this point. One of my mates was getting louder by the minute with all the alcohol we had consumed. "Let's play for 50 dollars," the guy said. I didn't have that kind of money on me but before I could reply my mate said "Yeah, we'll play for fofty Dollars. We will kick your ass." I started to feel the cold around me, it was a dark feeling and it scared me.

As we continued to win potting ball after ball, I could see the other two guys were getting angry. I could see very tall dark shadows hovering around these guys. I felt real ill at this point. I was saying "Sure let's just not play for money. It's only a bit of craic." Next thing I know my mate pots the wining ball. It's all over. We had won.

The two guys we were playing were so pissed off. "I'm going to cut your head off you Irish bastard." I was trying to reason with them.

I wasn't long sobering up after that. "You cheated and you're going to pay," he ranted. My mate was at the bar and didn't see this happening. I was trying desperately to get his attention. It was like I was stuck in a time warp. I tried to reason with the guys saying I didn't want to fight and we didn't cheat. "What if we give you your money back?" I offered. "No, we have been waiting for the chance to get you," he snarled. I'm in sheer terror at this point, but I was ready to stand up for myself.

I see these tall dark shadows making their way towards me. They blocked out everything else. Next thing a bottle came towards me and smashed beside me. I was in the middle of a bar fight, it was like something out of a John Wayne movie! The fight was starting to spread around the bar. More people were getting involved. "The police are on their way," the bar man shouted. I was in a scuffle when I saw a flash of light by the door. I heard a gentle voice saying "leave now." I ran out of the bar like Forest Gump. I ran down small streets to get away. I could hear the police cars in the distance. I thought *feck me, I'm in big trouble.* I noticed a police car coming towards me so I jumped a fence and start running through the back of these buildings, jumping fences as I ran.

I ended up on a back street. I ducked behind a wall when I heard a car approaching me. I heard my named being called. It was one of mates from the bar. I got into the back seat and they covered me with jackets. *What would my aunt and uncle think? I'm not a troublemaker?* I felt so sick. "Stop the car, stop the car," I shouted. They pulled over and I vomited out the side of the car.

We arrived at my aunt and uncles house. They pulled the car in quickly and let me out before speeding off. I was standing at the back door trying to sober up, thinking about what I was going to say if they were still up. I made my way in the door and everyone was sleeping. I got to the door at the top of the basement and I noticed a tarot card lying on the floor. When I looked at it something clicked inside me. It was a movie of my future and I could see everything so clearly. It was so dark. It was unimaginable and scared the living hell out me. I saw myself in the darkest place I had ever imagined. My loved ones were not there, I was alone. If this was a glimpse of what my future could be *Oh MY GOD please never send me there* I thought. I broke down crying. I cried so hard I began whaling like a banshee! I woke up everyone in the house. Tammy and Brian came running out of their bedroom to see what on earth was going on. I wasn't making any sense, the tears dripped down my face. Bless them, they must have really thought that I had lost the plot. All I could do was point at the card and say, "my life, my life." They got me a coffee. Brian stayed up for a while sharing his words of wisdom with me. He said "Robbie, drinking will only bring you away from the light that you are. It attracts all the darkness that you are also. You are very special. It's time to become a man and start making the right decisions about your life."

The next day I felt horrible. I had the hangover from hell. I was in a dark place again. At breakfast that morning I was grumpy with the kids taking my crap out on them, which wasn't very fair as all they showed me was unconditional love. Tammy looked annoyed but she didn't say anything. She took the kids and went off for the day. I felt so bad and guilty inside. Brian had some sort of an understanding and went easy on me.

When Tammy came back that evening she told us there was a big fight in a bar last night in town. *Oh crap.* I piped up and said that it was me, I was there, I was drinking whiskey thinking I could keep up with these guys, but I couldn't. "I'm really sorry for everything. I didn't mean to cause any trouble. I'm sorry if I was off with the kids, I love them," I said. "It's okay" Tammy said. For me, this was a point in my life where I felt loved and I knew they really cared for me. I made the decision to stop drinking because when I drank I didn't know the cut-off point. Drinking was my sticky plaster, it would not help me to grow and heal. How I had seen myself in that tarot card, the movie I got to see of how I could be, wasn't what I wanted my life to be like. I wanted a happy life full of love.

14

The Book on the Floor Is Calling Me, *'Read Me Robbie, Read Me'*

The book Tammy wanted me to read lay on the floor of my bedroom. Well, you'll never guess what? The book started to call me. I know this may sound really funny or even hard to believe, so you can imagine what was going through my head! Every single night I would go to bed and as I lay down to go sleep the book would call out to me *"Read me. Robbie, read me"*. This was yet another moment of the craziness. I was fighting the urge so hard not to read it and yet the magnetism of the book intensified. One evening I couldn't block out the sound of the book anymore, the feelings inside me were so strong that I had to see what was in this book. It would be the first ever spiritual book I would read, in fact it was actually the first book I had ever read in my life! I picked up the book and opened the first page.

The book was about a Medium that could commutate with the Spirit world. As I began to read that night it felt as if I was starting to read a book about my life. For the first time ever, a moment of true awakening took place to answer my many deep questions. It was like looking at my life as a blurry picture and then it started to become clear, like all the darkness had been lifted. In that moment I felt every positive emotion throughout my body, I was buzzing.

I was hooked! I read into the early hours of the morning. I was a slow reader and because this was the first ever book I had read, I needed to read back through things a couple of times until it made sense, then I would fall asleep. I woke the next morning and didn't go up for breakfast. I started reading again. It really felt like it was my life I was reading about. I felt a real connection. I'm alive! It was like being awakened from a deep dream. Finally my life was starting to make sense. This was my first ever light-bulb moment. I couldn't put the book down.

Brian thought I was on hunger strike! I wouldn't be one to miss out on food so I decided to join them for breakfast, book in hand. When Brian and Tammy saw the book their face's lit up. They looked so happy. "I see you started reading," Brian said. Deep down inside the fire within my soul was alight and burning. I spent the next couple of days immersed in the book not wanting to put it down. I was reading from the moment I would waken to the moment I fell asleep. Brian and Tammy didn't see much of me during this time. They must have thought I had become a hermit! I learned from this book that the experiences the Medium had were so similar to mine. It felt as if he had written the book especially for me. All of the things I was seeing and feeling as a child, a teenager and a young adult were now making sense—there was a higher reason for this. Because I never questioned my experiences during my childhood, my sense of purity prevailed. Then as a teen I closed down completely and pushed it away as a coping mechanism. Being the young adult I was so lost in all these other realities of life. I had no understanding or had anyone to help me understand.

As I read through the book it talked about Spirits and Spirit Guides, Angels and healing, which were all the things I had been experiencing. This was the first part of the jigsaw of my life. I decided to clear my bedside locker as I felt the need to put the things that meant the most to me there, like a little alter. I was asking lots of questions in my mind as you can imagine. I wanted the answers to why I was seeing things all my life? Why was I so sensitive to people, their emotions and their energy? Why was I hearing voices in my head? I wanted to see through the veil of illusion. I WAS LOOKING FOR THE VALIDATION TO MY LIFE.

As it came close to the end of the book it sparked the biggest question I had ever asked myself. I felt so angry and hurt with God, the Angels and the Spirit world. I asked a direct question to nothing or no-one else but GOD;

GOD, WHY HAVE YOU ABANDONED ME?

Is this world a big joke? Because if it is I must be the only one who is not laughing or missed the joke!

GOD, I'm so confused and angry. I read this book—it's opened me up and joined some of the dots, yet I feel now I'm losing all faith and I can't validate my life?

Are you real, GOD? Are you real, GOD? PLEASE SHOW ME A SIGN.

GOD, can you hear me. I'm screaming in my mind and from the depths of soul crying for an answer. PLEASE SHOW ME A SIGN.

I'm looking for evidence. I need it to go on, to give my life worth meaning, not meaningless, to fill the void of darkness to light.

From this day my conversation with God started. I was asking God with every single thought I had and at every single moment. I never stopped asking.

Are you real? If so, show yourself to me?

Can you hear me GOD? I screamed with all my anger at that moment.

Send me a sign. I need a sign.

I then started asking everyone I could think of in heaven to send me a sign.

Please, I need something to make this real for me.

I was asking my grandfather to come through to me and help me. I have to say this was part of my discipline and would help me greatly when the time came for me to fully step into my power. I would sit chatting with Brian and Tammy whilst in a full conversation with God and the spirit world. My mind never stopped searching for the answers. When I was in my bedroom alone I would speak out loud until I fell asleep. I was desperate for a validation that would give my life a sense of purpose and meaning. At this time I was reflecting on lots of different parts of my life. I was doing the one thing I have always done to myself and that was beat myself up. I was thinking of my family and how much I loved them, yet I looked back on my life at all the disharmony we had experienced.

Brian got me another job this time in a local service station. I was a gasoline attendant. It was great because it gave me some independence. The guy that owned the garage was from the Lebanon and was a real sound boss. I would put gas into the cars and I looked after the shop.

The weather was starting to get cold so I was wearing my brand new snow gear. Even though there was no snow it could get windy on the garage forecourt and when I was doing eight-hour shifts it could get very cold. The cold made my body feel sore and tired from my fourth of July accident injuries, but I was managing. I felt settled for the first time in a long time. I felt I belonged somewhere and my relationship with Brian and Tammy was truly special. They were like my spiritual teachers guiding me and showing me towards my true life path.

Brian had gone to see this guy who was a Medium and my grandfather came through to him. Brian felt that if I went to see this Medium it would help me so much, but I just wasn't ready yet. Even though I was going through my many experiences I was still so sceptical. All I could think about was *how could he tell me anything about my life?* I wanted God to validate my life as I didn't feel a Medium could bring me the answers I craved.

15

How I Met My Gauridian Angel

22-11-2002—The Day God Sent Me My Sign

My Guardian Angel—a sign from God. This would be the day I would find my true-life's path and God would give me back my faith. This time it would be sealed within the very seat of my soul. From this day on I would never be in a place of fear. The foundation would be set— seeing the person I was born to be.

I was born to shine, just like you! It would be my path in this lifetime to bring the light of unconditional love to the souls that needed me to help them ... to be of service to the love and light of God.

Only through my darkness could I find my light.

(Song—*Nobody Knows* Paul Brady)

I woke up and the morning was still. I started my day by asking God to bring me a SIGN. It was cold outside so I put on my snow gear. I went up-stairs for some breakfast before my morning shift. I felt happy. The day felt different. I can't explain it. My aunt Tammy is the best cook ever and would always have something special for my breakfast. She made me a packed lunch every day for work. They really did spoil me. I was just like their own kids only I was a twenty-something year old kid! I loved it all the same. I had started to think about Christmas— it was only around the corner. My thoughts turned to my family. I don't know why but Christmas wouldn't be my favourite time of the year, yet I was looking forward to spending it with Brian and Tammy and their kids.

Where I worked was only a five minute walk from my home so I would usually leave about 10 minutes before my shift started. As I finished up my breakfast the house started to get busy with the kids.

My aunt looked after another couple of kids so it would be all go for her at this time of the morning. I grabbed my coat and headed out the front door shouting back to them "See you later!" As I walked to work I was thinking about my life yet again, wondering if this lost feeling would ever go away. I asked GOD *where am I going? Are you real? Please tell me? What is my purpose?*

When I arrived at work my boss had already opened up. He wasn't going to stay for long as he had a busy morning. He gave me my till float for the day and left. The morning was slow but I didn't mind. I would juggle between the pumps and the shop. I was getting used to seeing the familiar faces that stopped for fuel. Most of them were regulars as the garage always seemed to be the best price around. When that garage got busy it was really busy. I got good tips which my boss found funny because it wasn't really something that people would normally do. I wasn't complaining though! The extra cash came in handy. The morning was passing by so fast. I had a good steady flow coming in and out of the garage. Then out of nowhere it got very busy. I was ran off my feet. My boss came back which was unusual. He said he was driving by, saw how busy it was and decided to stop and give me a hand. He took some cash off me as there was no safe. I could be carrying a couple of thousand dollars or more at any given time. He hung round for about twenty minutes until things quietened down and off he went.

The petrol pumps were old and dated. If you can imagine, the pumps had three different speeds, five, ten, and fifteen. The fuel would pump faster or slower depending on what speed the pump was set at. I would set the pump speed for the amount of fuel going in so I could keep all the cars moving at a steady pace. I was at full steam ahead. I remember my ankle and neck were a little sore from the cold weather. I was soldiering on though—a good auld hard working Irish spirit! I was standing in the centre of the island where the pumps were. In the middle of the busyness I remember this particular car pulling in because all the other cars were new and modern. This car was a long car, a brown estate and unlike the other cars it was older. It pulled into the front pump on the left hand side.

My mind was focused on getting all the cars filled as quickly as possible. I made my way around to the driver's window to ask how much they wanted me to put in. I remember thinking that the old estate car looked in perfect condition. The paintwork was like new.

The window opened really slowly but not fully. I first heard this very softly spoken voice from the lady "can you put twenty dollars in please?" She had this glow about her. I rushed round to open the cap to put the pump in. A warm feeling started to come over me but in the busyness of the station I didn't have time to think about it fully. I went to attend to the other cars, some of which were getting a full tank, which would take longer compared to just twenty dollars. As I stood waiting on the cars to get filled up, all of a sudden they were all done and it was just me and the brown estate at the front pump. There was a silence, it was weird. I took the pump out of the brown estate, locked the cap and started to make my way back around to the window. I tapped the window and waited for it to come down. The lady looked old yet had the youngest face, not a line or a wrinkle, so vibrant was the light beaming from her, so pure. She was glowing. Her hair was so white—a picture of pure perfection. This lady had so much beauty, like the face of a young girl, but the body of an older lady. I asked her for the money for the fuel and as I reached into the car she took my hand by the wrist. I panicked a little and went to pull back, but at the same time she held me by the wrist. I had this over whelming sense of peace come over me. I can't explain the connection I was feeling. My whole body felt like it was plugged into the universe, it was amazing, very overwhelming yet a real sense of calm. I was talking to myself in my head, *what is happening? I really feel like crying, but I feel so safe, so connected to this lady. Am I in twilight zone?* I asked myself. I stopped trying to pull back and then she spoke to me again in the softest voice ever. I looked into her eyes. Her eyes were like no other eyes I had ever seen—they were full of love, light and purity. She looked right into my soul. Her light reminded me of things I had seen before in the past and as a child. She glowed and emanated.

"Robert, don't worry you are safe," she said.

How does she know my name?

"I came here today to see you," she continued.

"What do you mean?" I asked. She let go of my wrist softly.

"We have heard you. Your call has been answered."

I'd say the look on my face was priceless! I was shocked and stunned. I was having this surreal experience with no shadows, voices, or flashes, just this amazing light coming from this lady.

"You have been asking for a SIGN."

I nodded yes. Oh my God, I am hopping out of my skin!

"I came here today to bring you your SIGN."

She then reached over and picked up this old piece of purple and red cloth, turned towards me and opened it. She took out a coin, there is a cross cut from the centre of the coin. She placed it in my hand.

"Here is your SIGN. This coin comes from us, a message from heaven. This coin represents your strength and faith—all the things that you are. I came today to help you, to bring you the message of HOPE. This coin has come to you so you can help many people."

"I am your Guardian Angel, Robert, sent by God. I have manifested to you in this way because if it was any other shape or form you would not have been able to understand, so this is the easiest way for you to understand me in the physical. I have been with you since the beginning of time, always by your side and I came today to show you your true path just like you have asked for and to tell you we are real."

I was in shock. Shock that this was real. I had been screaming with every thought in my mind, body and soul for a SIGN and now my Guardian Angel was here, crossed over into physical and this was so real. OH MY GOD!

"God has made this happen. It's time to put your faith back in God and the Angels. God's love for you will never change no matter how angry you think you are. God will never deny you. Your anger has brought you to a place of feeling lost and hurt. Your anger attracts the darkness that you are, but you are also light. There have been many bridges to cross in your lifetime. What I have to tell you so you can tell others, is that we have never abandoned you, nor have we ever abandoned anyone else. We are always there with you all from the highest high to the lowest low, helping and guiding, this is the way it has and always will be."

She continued ...

"We are the silent workers. It's not our job to be visible to all at every moment, even though we are always helping. You have chosen to live on this plain, earth as you call it, so you can experience this life through the physical and the emotional, thus helping you to learn the lessons of the soul, the lessons of love and compassion, the lesson of kindness and forgiveness, giving and receiving. We are here to guide you but I am your Guardian Angel. I am your gatekeeper. I have a very different job to other Angels. I act like the filter for you, keeping you safe along your journey, only intervening with the will of your free will, or the will of your soul's agreement. I have been with you for many life times, you have been mostly asleep in this one, and up until this point it has been your soul's agreement so you could work through your karma. I will help you to remember everything, but that will come in time. You will receive all the answers you seek and you will be able to bring wisdom from other life times to this one helping you and others."

"Will I really?"

"Yes."

"I will be with you even more now along with other Angels and Spirit Guides—just like it is for all the other souls on this earth. They too have got Angels helping them, there is not one soul more special here than another. God has no favourites—God's love is equal in heaven and on earth. God's love is vast beyond your thinking. It's time for you to understand there is no greater gift than the gift of life. The answer you are seeking here is service and how best to serve. The understanding will come for this as you find yourself again and open the wisdom of your heart."

"Okay," I said because I had little understanding of the wisdom of my heart.

"We are unconditional love and that is even an understatement. There are no real words that can describe us Angelic beings as we come from a place on high."

"I came to tell you to look deep into your heart and soul for you will find the answer. You already know it's time to awaken and you will help souls on this plain/earth to wake up as this is your gift. You will remember who and where you came from and then you will help others to remember."

I was stunned. All this has happened as I stood in the forecourt of a garage. My Guardian Angel had just manifested to me in the physical. I knew I was part of it yet I felt like I was not, it was like a movie playing. I had the lead part but not in it if you get me, it was very surreal.

I was listening intently to every word she said, feeling these massive waves of love and healing. It was like I was a computer that crashed and had just gotten a reboot and was getting new software. I was getting the blue prints for this lifetime.

Her amazing glow was indescribable. She looked like complete and utter perfection.

She continued ...

"You have had free will from the moment you came onto this earth. But it's your soul's journey or agreement to meet me today, this was chosen before you entered this plain."

"What do you mean?" I asked.

"It's time to listen dear one. You have many gifts that you brought here, you can use them for good or evil. This will be your free will and choice but I will never leave your side, in darkness or light."

"I don't want to be dark. I want to be free of all the things that weigh me down, all the hurts and pains," I pleaded.

"These things are all part of your experience and you choose how you face them. You can either face them with love or hate but there will never be a time of not facing them. You all have to see your shadows. Choice and free will is the world's biggest gift. Accepting responsibility is what you have to do. This will help to set you free."

"Responsibility?"

"Yes, responsibility. For every single thought, action, feeling and emotion, happy or sad as these are your own thoughts and have never been our thoughts or the making of heaven. They have been the making of man and woman. By taking responsibility for these things, you take responsibility for your own creations and not the creations of others."

"I came to awaken you with the love you are. You are very gifted but a powerful healer. You won't understand this for some time though. The feelings and visions that you have been experiencing all your life are very real. I am the validation sent to you from heaven. You have been seeing and sensing things around you from you were a child. That was us, but you were also sensing darkness—you had to see both sides to fulfil this lifetime's journey.

"From a child you could see the darkness around people. You were so sensitive, this is why you had so much anger and could not control it, but you also saw the light and from a child you have been helping souls. Your mother will be the answer to this. You will have to speak to her, as your mother holds the key to this and understands. Your mother is also gifted. She will help you understand your past and why things were the way they were so you can unlock some of your childhood memories."

"What happened to me? I can't remember much of my childhood, but when I do it's like I have this energy going through me like a million volts that I cannot control." I asked.

"Yes, the answers for this will come but not today dear one. I have been watching over you and guiding you towards this day. I will help you to understand all which is you. Choosing before you came here to work on your karma and then to help others, bringing them HOPE and teaching them about unconditional love and forgiveness. You will help people to learn how to heal themselves, helping them to see the light that is within them, bringing them back to the great central sun of Mother and Father God, the great I Am That I am.

You will have to work on your gifts as they will not all come easy. Learning to harness them first and then there will come a time when they will be in your memory as if they had never left you so you can teach others to remember theirs.

Every soul can connect to God, their Guardian Angel, Angels and the Spirit family as there is no separation. You all have your own unique way to connect and no man or woman has a greater gift than the other. You are all gifted.

From this day on our connection is sealed. I am with you at every moment to help you, protect you, and there will be many more Angels and Spirit guides who will come to you to help you understand about your gifts, fine-tuning them. Not every guide or Angel will come from the other side. You will meet people on your journey in the physical that will also help you, they are called Earth Angels. You will also work with masters."

"What are masters?" I asked, not having a clue there was such a thing. If I was honest I wasn't the worlds most clued in person about Angels or Guardian Angels. So the whole masters thing went right over my head, just like it was meant to and I didn't get my answer about them then and there.

"How can I do this?"

"Your life's purpose is to work with the Angels and Spirit realms. Communicating with us, learning to talk about the truth and living in it, helping others to see their truth. We will send the people but only when the timing is right. Learning to walk before you can run, the art of mindfulness. It will take so much discipline and it will not be handed to you or be easy as you have also chosen this lesson. Do not give up. It will become easier as time grows.

Remember be humble, focus on service. I have told you GOD has not one favourite, nor does God give someone more than the other. Be humble for the life you live and your life will be abundant. It's not about shouting out and naming your gifts, it's about living in them, the truth of them and walking in honest shoes. You will also have to learn this lesson again but don't give up as the answers will come as you need them. Knock and the door will open; seek and you shall find."

"But how can I do all of this? I will never be able to do all this?"

"Faith dear one. The road is your journey. Have patience as I tell you I was with you every step of the way from birth to this point. I have been with you at every experience. I know you want all the answers. The answers for you are not just ready to come but they will in time when you speak to your mother. You must learn patience. You can't have everything now or your life would have no meaning. Your life will unfold like the lotus flower revealing something new all the time. Have patience—all good things come to those who wait.

I was with you New Year's Eve in your apartment. I saw your pain as you looked into the mirror. You felt so lost and alone. We took you out of your body and back to the nightclub when you were high on drugs to the night you lost your teeth and then saw us. We took you back so you could see your light, so you could see our presence as we watched over you."

"I don't know who I was back then," I replied. "After I knocked my teeth out that night I saw you all around the people in the club, I knew it was real but I was in so much darkness that I suppressed this."

"We know. We brought you back so you could see we were always there with you so you can look back and learn," she confirmed.

"When I stood crying in the mirror that night I know I was taken back by you to see the night club, to see you by my side and see all the other angels around people. I closed back down after I came back to my apartment. Why have I had so much fear about you? I don't understand?" I asked.

"All you hold is locked deep within your mind, it will take time for you to understand. We promise you will receive every answer, some may be very hard to understand and some won't. As I have already told you, take responsibly, it's part of your growth. Love is and will always be the only one true answer. To thyne self always be true."

"Who writes the rules I am living in?" I enquire.

"You do! Free will can take you on many journeys, its' time to start living by this. If you can think it, dream it, feel it, see it, then you can be it! You are the creator of your own thoughts. You can live in darkness or in light as you have chosen in your past. It's your past that will shape you for the future. This has enabled you to learn who you are again, all part of your plan."

"My plan?"

"Your plan or path hasn't been God's will or our will that has chosen your lifetime or lessons, it has been thee will, the journey of the soul. Do you understand?"

"So I am choosing everything?"

"Yes, so be careful for what you wish for or what you wish upon others. Live by the ones who have come before you, and their great teachings. Be kind, be loving, be humble, be compassionate. Respect yourself and others and they will respect you.

Forgive and you will be forgiven.

Hate and hate will be you.

An act of kindness will far exceed any other act coming from a place of love.

Give but not to receive. When you give from free will not to receive, this is when you will most receive.

These are only simple teachings but they have the most meaning. People have forgotten to live this way which is why there is so much disharmony.

Do you remember the train ride when you were arrested?"

"Yes," I quietly replied.

"I have always been with you.

Before you went down the flight of stairs at the train station you heard the words, *SLOW DOWN*. That was me, helping you, guiding you, but you were not open or did not know how to trust. We have been trying to help you find a place of trust—it has taken many knocks and bangs for you. It was not your time to leave America but we were just trying to help you to listen. When the police officer arrested you we surrounded you with light that day and kept you safe—we also brought other help into your life."

Oh my God I thought of my friend, John, the police officer who gave me the P B A card in case I ever got stopped. "Did you help with this too?"

"Yes, that was I."

"I heard you that day but I thought it was mind talking just like other times."

"We know. You have been a hard one to awaken.

We can and do communicate to the mind through thought form, it's just people don't listen. When they do, they don't trust because they are becoming so desensitised. We are communicating with everyone, some have just learned to tune in more and it will now be your time again.

Dear one we have always been with you. There have been many helpers that have come to you throughout your life so far.

I have to tell you that the night of the accident, Independence Day, when you were down by the beach, you had many Angels with you, helping you with all the other people, there was much light there. I was with you that night as you lay pinned to the floor. You have been feeling my presence from a child but that night I really allowed you to feel the energy. I am your assigned gatekeeper, a job given to me by God, it will always be my job to protect, guide and watch over you dear one. So when you lay there, you came out of your body, it was a job to watch over you as this too was not your time. You had some spirit family there too."

As she told me this it was like I had just remembered that part of the accident. When I heard the bang, I was gone. The first thing in my memory was my Grandfather which gave me a feeling of being safe or protected.

"Yes, that was he helping you also. He will help you so much from now."

This really knocked me for six. "My grandfather was really there?"

"Yes, Paddy your Grandfather. So the reason for this accident was to finally push you to a place where you would let go of your demons that you have had since a child.

It is never God's aim to hurt but the soul's journey is to let go and find oneness so they can stand in the unity of Mother and Father God, the great I AM presence. You have also come into this world with demons to release and heal the wounds of your past paths. What you couldn't see at this time was your light and how much you were loved, so you subconsciously started to revert to your darkness.

This is when the dark soul of the night would start to impress on you. We were sending and showering you in much light but you could not see, the veil was truly covering you. So as you spent the next few weeks slipping away, it was your ego mind that had given up and was very much controlling how you moved forward. Free will is always there and we cannot and will not intervene outside of spiritual or universal laws as it's written. I could see your light diminish and as it did so you started to disconnect from your soul.

I never left you. Do you understand?"

"I know now," I said.

She kept reinforcing all the time that she was with me. That felt so comforting, it really put me into a place of ease like never before. *This is totally amazing. I am having a conversation with my Guardian Angel. Quick pinch yourself—my life has meaning!*

"Dear one there has always been love around you, but you had chosen to go to the depths of your darkness to find your light. How far you would go was up to you and your free will."

"So only through my darkness could I find my light?"

"Yes, this is true."

My Guardian Angel surrounded me in her pure unconditional love at every moment of this conversation.

I had a life that I should be so grateful for yet I had lost all sight and sound of what was important. I was so grateful in this moment. *Thank you God.*

Then we spoke about me trying to kill myself.

"I was with you more in your time of need than ever before. You needed me because you had chosen your darkness—the dark soul of the night was upon you."

I could feel myself welling up thinking of that night as she spoke.

"The universe will always give you what you focus on most. When your sister left for home and you had chosen to stay and end your life, I was still by your side."

"All I could see was the darkness. I couldn't see the light and as the dark soul of the night called, I saw it, I felt it took me piece by piece. I was listening," I replied.

"Yes, it was at this time you only had one particle of light within you. The rest was darkness. We never stopped shining light on you."

"I didn't know how to handle my emotions. I just wanted to die. I felt I had nothing to live for. I felt I had no meaning," I cried.

"It's okay, don't worry, we come not to judge. There is no measure for greatness to which you and I come from. God does not condemn you. God loves you—every atom and molecule is their greatest creation. You will help others to heal and find the power within them.

God has a plan and for every single soul that walks this earth. God has not created your pain because this will be the will of man. God has given you the tools you need to fulfil your destiny. Learning to use the tools in a place of love not the ego where love cannot exist, will be your challenge."

"Dear one on the night you tried to take your life your soul cried out to the heavens. The darkness had its grip on you, it was then God intervened. Because your soul cried from such depths of despair for forgiveness and love, I was given permission to intervene to save your soul. This was not like other times."

I said "I remember crying, feeling angry and hurt. I took the tablets and drink. I felt like a lost soul and nothing else existed. I started to drift in and out of consciousness that night. I remember looking at my mother's painting of Christ's hands and thinking *what have I done?* Screaming out "PLEASE SAVE ME. PLEASE FORGIVE FOR I KNOW NOT WHAT I DO. The next thing I wake up with the phone in my hand."

"Yes, that was me. I intervened divinely and helped with the permission of your soul and God, it was the only way I could. It was me who got the phone and phoned your uncle. It was me who kept you safe from your darkness. That was the last time you will ever be in that place. You have released the karma to the light, for a place of love. It is love that will conquer all."

"My room was so bright. That was you?"

"Yes, the light was I and your other helpers."

"What am I?'

"You are that which comes from the most perfect thing you will ever know and the love from this is endless. You are an infinite being just like your creator, never ending; you are all that there is."

There was so much information to take in. *How will I remember everything?* I reminded myself that I was on the garage forecourt. Time stood still. As my mind started to wonder she said "don't worry dear one, you will remember."

I was amazed at every moment. I felt so alive, thinking *my life is not going to be the same after this.* Inside saying to myself, *I want to be free.*

"In time you will be free. You will grow and your wisdom will grow to set you and others free.

You were really thinking about your mother. It was us that played her song on the radio to let you know the love she has for you."

"What? You can play songs on the radio?"

"Yes, one of the many things we do, we have been sending signs to you throughout your life, just like we have for all the other souls on this earth. The time is coming where people will understand and wake up. But you must pay attention and watch for the signs as they are not always the big picture you envision them, as they can be as subtle as the smell of a flower or the sound of a song or a tiny feather. There will always be signs."

She continued ...

"There is no separation, every single thing is connected. There are many angels working on this earth at this moment and there will be more to come as things change.

Your mother is going through a lot of pain, she carries lots of hurt. She is and always will be your greatest teacher. You chose her to learn forgiveness and unconditional love, tough lessons. Your mother loves you dearly and you think of her all the time. You will both, one day find balance and she will see your light. Don't worry she will be fine."

I felt so emotional at this moment.

"You will doubt life still after I leave today as it's nearly my time to go."

"I won't. I promise I won't."

She smiled and said, "it's okay, you have your faith back now and that will never leave you again, your coin for this is your soul's true awakening.

There will be people who will come into your life, your spiritual journey, who will try and hurt you. They will not understand you and they will try to destroy your good name. Remember it is your light that they see, not your darkness—it's your light they will most fear."

"What do you mean by this, please tell me?"

She never answered me just smiled in the most loving way.

I wasn't ready to hear the answer or maybe I had to go through the experience to really understand, so I thought time would tell.

"There will be some challenges you have to face dear one. There will be one major lesson. You really need to listen now.

Remember who you really are, not what they want you to become or what they will say. You will meet the dark soul of the night once more, but not like before. This time you will know thee self. It will be from a place that all can see. You will tread in your old shoes again and be on and off your path, but don't fear we will never leave you."

"No," I pleaded. "I don't want to go there again."

"It won't be the same. Forgiveness will be the only answer—hold no judgement. This is what will finally bring you to your soul, the three-fold flame of your heart. The flame of GOD that burns within each and every one of you.

By 2009 you will never look back—this will be your time. Remember to write—keep a dairy at all times. This is very important that you hear this."

"Yes," I agreed.

"There will come a time where they will become your books. They will be your salvation but also the guide for your books. Use your writing as a channel from us on high."

"So I am writing books?" I questioned.

"Yes dear one, you will tell your story bringing the information we bring you. We will bring you a clear message to spread the message of HOPE. This world is coming into a place where there is and will be great changes. The world needs HOPE, the light of God and the love of God which is universal. It comes from a place of no attachment. God is real, you are real, and I AM THE VALIDATION OF THIS."

"Thanks so much," I said.

"It's my time to go now. I am guiding you now. I will be with you. Your coin will stay with you until one day it is your turn to come back, it will then come with you. Keep it safe as it is a special gift from heaven. It will bring healing to many—remember healing is your biggest gift."

"Will I ever see you again? Where do you live?" My rational and logical mind started to kick in. *I am after meeting my Guardian Angel who crossed over to the physical, brought me a gift, told me all the things I am and I ask her does she live close to me! How silly am I?* I had just received all the proof of validation I had asked for, yet I couldn't help but doubt what had just happened.

With that she pulled out of the garage and was gone.

(Song—*Goo Goo Dolls* Iris—From the movie "City of Angels")

I was buzzing. If anyone could have seen me, dancing and jumping around the forecourt of the garage like I had just won the lotto! I do often tell people that I did win the lotto. It was the lotto of my life, my coin, Guardian Angel, my prize. My life and God were my biggest gifts of all.

God, you have answered my call, and this is not the first time. Thank you so much God. I love you. This world is real and there is life after life. I have a purpose, a meaning. What a day, I can't wait to go home and tell Brian and Tammy!

I waited for my shift to end which felt like an eternity! All I could think about was what had just happened. I have dreamt many things but this was surreal! My Guardian Angel crossed over to the physical plane and gave me a coin. I waited for my shift to end holding my coin, it was electric! I was buzzing with excitement for my life. God heard and answered me.

I ran home after my shift ended. I burst through the door like a mad man ranting about how I just met my Guardian Angel. Brian and Tammy thought I was crazy! I was the one who had been asking God for the sign, not Brian and Tammy, so they looked at me as if I had two heads! I can totally understand why because I wasn't explaining

it too well with all my excitement. I went to my room and spent a
few hours in silence. I started doubting then, listening to my ego
asking was it real? This miracle had just happened to me. I started to
question this and all my fears and insecurities kept coming up. *What
if they don't believe me?* My room was the stillest ever, no flashes,
shadows or lights. I went back upstairs that evening for dinner and
spoke to Brain and Tammy. I explained what I had experienced that
day, and as I started to talk in more detail they were in as much shock
as I was.

For some strange reason my ego mind was working hard on me.
I spoke to Brian about this as I felt it was coming from a place of
doubt. Brian explained to me about EGO and its meaning. He told me
this meant *E= Ease G= God O= Out—Ego.* I would have to learn to
still my mind and thoughts. Brian thought that meditation would be
a good place to start. I never meditated in my life so this was all very
new to me. I was only at the start of my new journey, my awakening.

I cleared off some space on my bedside locker at the side of my
bed. This became my Angel alter, a sacred space. Brian told me to
take the time to connect, that this would help me. I was also reading
a new book and this reinforced what Brian was telling me. Before
I met my Guardian Angel, I was having all these experiences when
I went to bed at night, now there was complete silence! I was trying to
understand everything my Guardian Angel had told me. I continued the
conversation in my mind, but there was silence, no shadows, or lights,
or anything being moved around my room.

I started to write. I would go to bed at the same time every evening
to begin my ritual. I would light a candle and breathe deeply to relax
my body and mind. I would place my hands on my body—the heat
generated from this was extraordinary, like an oven! I remembered the
heat from the lady that helped me before I came to America, only my
hands were so much hotter. It felt as if someone had lit a fire on them.

I would place my hands on different parts of my body and the ease
and relief I felt was profound. I would later discover these were my
chakras and I was self-healing. My Guardian Angel had told me I
would be a healer. *Is this what she meant?* I was in a routine. I think

I was trying to force it, but the silence still continued. The doubting 'Thomas' within was working hard. I was back in my rational mind.

Every day at work I asked the locals if they had ever seen this car my Guardian Angel was driving or if they knew this lady. Guess what? Not one person knew her or her car! I was desperate for answers. I thought meeting her that day would change my life there and then, like hey presto everything would be in harmony!

I felt myself getting pissed off and angry. I was feeling very frustrated. I wanted it all there and then. I hadn't listened to what she had told me. Patience is what she told me *"when the time is right I am always with you."* I was trying so hard to see with my physical eyes and this was totally blocking my mind. I would spend my time writing in my diary. Looking back, I can see now how the writing helped me to release my anger. The things I wrote in my first diary were so dark, but as my Guardian Angel had told me, this would help me find myself. I was letting go, clearing the past so I could make way for the present.

I stopped asking at the garage about this lady, not confiding in anyone it was my Guardian Angel. I knew in my heart it was my Gatekeeper and my coin was my validation. When I held it I could feel her connection from it. I would hold it at night as I meditated.

Brian and I had a deep conversation. He told me he could see my gifts but I was still blinded. He also said that one day I would work with the Angels and when I opened up the whole universe would open up for me. I could not see this. I felt the silence was my enemy, what I failed to see was that silence was my ally.

I went to my sacred space at the same time every evening. I began reading and questioning, *why all this silence?*

Brian and I were messing around with a set of tarot cards one day. We would start by spreading the cards out in front of us, picking one and reading the instructions in the book to give each other readings. It was good fun but I was reading from the book not my psychic ability, sure it was all harmless fun.

Brian recommended I go to see a Medium he knew. I agreed but was totally sceptical. Everything at the beginning of my journey was coming from the left-brain. I was looking for solid concrete answers even though I had my coin. I became very rigid in my thoughts and this blocked me from sensing my Angels.

The best advice Brian gave me was to learn how to control my gift. If I didn't I would crash and burn. I had to be patient. I agreed and I believed what he was saying. I thought it was only special people who had gifts. Even though my Angel told me there was no one soul more special than the other. I had lots of conflict at this time and this was part of the process of learning.

And let me tell you I was not special. I was as normal in my eyes as everyone else.

I went to my room that evening giving out again to the universe. I lay in bed in the candlelight. I placed my hands on my forehead and started to breathe slowly, in through my nose and out through my mouth. I felt myself drifting off into a semi-conscious state. I started to become aware of something else in my room. The feelings were back, the same as the day I had met my Guardian Angel. My senses heightened and my whole body became electrified. I took my hands away from my forehead and my candle started to flicker. It was glowing from one inch in height to about ten. My room was bathed in light and my body felt as if I had been plugged into the mains. I began to notice a very sharp ringing in my ears. It felt as if there was someone screaming at a frequency I had never heard before.

I spent most of that night going through this experience. When I woke up the next day I knew things would never be the same. I spent three full days in the house going through a massive body cleanse. I must have visited the bathroom over a hundred times in three days! It was as if my body had just experienced a massive shock.

My bedroom became my training ground. As I lay in bed, the light from the candle would start dancing. My room would fill with amazing colourful lights. The feeling had now elevated from 'plugged-into-the-mains' to the national grid, it was so intense!

My senses became so clear that I started to receive information. I was being downloaded with stuff that I had no knowledge of in this life. It was an amazing experience but I wasn't going out to tell the world. Things were changing and changing fast.

Brian started talking about a book he had just read. I would know exactly what he was talking about yet I had never seen any page of the book. I had this inner knowing. This was just some of the things I was experiencing.

I was seeing things clearer, like the light that was around people. I was receiving information, my whole body was a modem for it. I was seeing the shadows and outlines again. Then I would receive the information which was coming from my Guardian Angel. These colours were Angels. I had seen these colours before. I saw these colours the night of the accident at the nightclub and also at other places in my life. The shadows or silhouettes were Spirit. I would share some of my experiences with Brian and Tammy. They had read many books so they sort of knew what was going on.

The one thing that stood to me was I never once stopped talking to my Angels in my mind or even out loud. If I didn't get the answer direct I kept up the conversation, I was very disciplined. I was downstairs this one day. Tammy called me to help her with something so I went to help her. I could sense this feeling, like an energy coming from the kid's bedroom. Tammy didn't sense it. The next thing we hear a real loud bang. We both ran into the bedroom, it was ice cold. We stood facing each other, all of a sudden this Spirit walked right in between us, it was about 6 foot tall. Tammy's face was a picture! We both stood there. The hair stood on the back of my neck. Tammy said "Did you see that?" "Yes," I said. It walked right between us. Tammy couldn't believe her eyes. She asked me again if it was real. We could see through it, its shape, the full outline. It was transparent, amazing. We both couldn't wait to tell Brian. There was a lot of activity around the house so it was all fun for me anyway. I don't remember being afraid. I had no fear whatsoever. If anything, it was exciting! I wanted to see even more!

I was reading my book. It was talking about Spirit Guides and how these beings had a totally different job to Angels, especially my Guardian Angel. I started asking my Spirit Guides to reveal themselves to me.

"Danny is My Name. I Am Your Spirit Guide"

I was sensing all the different energies between Angels and Spirits. For me I could feel a difference. This may not be the same for everyone but for me this was the way I felt them.

I was in my bedroom doing my usual routine of writing in my diary whilst asking questions in my head. I would ask very precise questions. I would call upon her, my Guardian Angel and then ask for my Spirit Guide's name. I was sitting up writing, asking, *what's your name? I can feel you.*

The ringing in my ears was so sharp. I kept asking. I felt the warmth, my Angel, the energy pulled back. I started to feel this light chill and a tingle on my face and hand. I ask again, *what is your name? Why won't you let me hear? Please tell me your name!* Next the sharp pitch stopped. I heard the name, Danny. It sounded like it was a mile away. I asked again, *is your name Danny?*

I heard it loud and clear "Danny is my name. I am your Spirit Guide sent to guide and help you." I nearly fell out of the bed. WOW, I had made my first audio connection! Instead of feeling and sensing I was now hearing my Pandora's box opening. My life was taking a turn towards the thing that was deep within me. I was living a life with purpose. I asked Danny lots of questions that night. He told me many things. He told me he could communicate in lots of different ways. We would not always communicate in audio, as it would be easier for him to communicate to my mind and thoughts just as my Angels did. He was going to help me understand this. I asked why I had so much heat from my hands?

"This heat is the energy of the universe. You channel it through your Angels. It comes from God given freely to each and every living being in this earth from the day you are born. You will use this energy to help others heal."

"Are you with me at every moment?" I asked.

"No, I only come when it is my time to work with you or you need my guidance."

I couldn't feel any others around me at that moment so I asked Danny were there any other Guides with me?

"Not at this time but there will be ones that will come and go for different life lessons, just like I will go when it's my time." "Will you not be my Guide forever?" I asked.

"No, I will be like your teacher and as you grow the teacher that matches that vibration for that growth will come. I too have to grow, I am also on a journey."

I thanked Danny for communicating with me but I could not see him at this time. I asked about my grandfather, Paddy.

"Very soon," he confirmed.

I was talking to them at every single moment and every thought. I cannot stress this enough. I would start off by calling God, my Guardian Angel, my Angels, my Spirit Guides, my family and friends of the Spirit world. When I did this I would imagine the sun how bright it was and then I would call them from a light a million times stronger. This definitely worked. It also gave this great sense of safety and security. I was very aware at this time to only call from this place, as I did not want to call upon lower vibration energies that had been with me in the past.

Things were shifting on for me on a spiritual level. On a human level I still had some obstacles. I hadn't spoken to Kim or my mother. The time was coming to face this. I felt I was stronger and was starting to understand the madness that I thought I was going through. I wasn't crazy. Everything happens for a reason. I knew this now. My battle with others thinking that I was crazy was still to come. At this point writing was a great outlay and helped me realise lots of different things. As I wrote about my feelings, they sounded so harsh at first, then started to lighten up and would later turn into forgiveness. I would find myself saying things like this ...

Quote from My First Dairy—2002

What is your pain? Pain, is it possible to turn it around? It will get hard if you fight with it, you will be surrounded with it. God, I surrender. I surrender, I surrender to my pain and I invoke myself in love, in love, in love to you God, for you God, with you God. Please let my pain be your love and turn into your love.

I would finish with thanking God, the universe, my Guardian Angel, my Angels, Spirit Guides, family, friends, and helpers.

I used my writing as a form of venting. This brought me to a whole new level of understanding, plus it taught me many things. When I wrote, the light of my Angels and Spirit friends always surrounded me.

I was learning to trust in what I was experiencing although at times I was still a bit sceptical about the world and other things, so when Brian mentioned again about going to see the Medium I finally agreed. Somewhere in my mind I was thinking *what could he tell me*? I didn't have much faith in others. I was very cautious. This was okay I told myself. I had just been through a major life changing experience. I was only starting to learn to love myself. I had many barriers and I didn't want to be hurt, so I kept the barriers and safety net up. Brian told me that the guy who was the Medium ran a circle. We would find out when it was on next and go. I was excited thinking about going.

I was lying in bed early one morning. I could feel my Spirit Guide in the room. It was 6.33 am. I started to wake up. I could feel the difference in the room temperature. I thought *this is weird* because I would always feel the warmth of my Angel first. I started asking questions in my mind. *How come I can't feel my angel?*

"You can," my Spirit guide replied. "The warmth is not in the room," was the next answer I got. "To feel within is more important than to sense outside, so look deep within and you will know us there."

I took a breath and as right as rain I could feel her. *But I can feel you in the room?*
"Yes you can."

This conversation is being done through my thoughts. It was Danny commutation with my mind and my Angel to my heart and all my emotions.

This is what they explained to me ...

"When your Guides come to you, you will not always feel them externally so start to become aware of what's happening inside."

What they told me was that my Guardian Angel, my Gatekeeper, would be the bridge to the other spirit realms and when my Guides would come she would be the one watching over me, "My filter", protecting but letting the Spirit realms do their duty.

What they explained next was very important.

"If you let your free-will be dark then this can also come. I can only protect you if you ask me and give me permission. This is why it's important to always come from a place of love and light and not hatred, the heart and not the ego mind. Do not get into the battle of ego. It has been said before there is no one more gifted than another and when you bring this message to the people there will be some who will understand but there will be many that will come from the place of the ego and therefore not realise that it is not them but the divine creator which is an aspect of them."

"What I am going to tell people or how can I show them this?"

"If you just be and come from a place of love, then this will shine through."

I asked Danny would he let me see him?

"When the time is right you will see me but don't focus on this," he answered.

Have you been in the situation when you think of the phone ringing and then it does and it's the person you're thinking of?

Later on that evening Brian, Tammy and the kids were going out. They asked if I would like to come with them. I wasn't really in the mood, I just wanted to chill so they headed off.

I had been thinking about Kim all day. I was lying stretched out on the living room chair daydreaming. I started to think about Kim. About a minute later the phone started ringing. When I answered it I realised it was Kim! My heart was in my mouth, I was shaking, she was crying. Understandably so she was very angry with me. I tried to explain that my head was in such a bad place, that I had lost all my identity. I didn't tell her that I tried to end my life. She wanted to know why I left. I said

I couldn't cope after the accident and when my sister left so I came up here.

"But why haven't you answered the phone?"

I couldn't answer her. "I am so sorry, Kim. I really am." I started to cry.

I knew I had hurt her so much after all the kindness she had shown me. I was after going through this whole experience, my world had been turned upside down and inside out.

"The person you knew then is not who I am now. I have changed. I have finally found myself through spirituality," I tried to explain.

Kim thought I had been brained-washed and was living in a cult. I couldn't articulate the words to say what I meant, only that I was sorry. She said that she was going out of her mind and how could I be so insensitive. I was caught up in this bubble at my aunt and uncles. I told Kim it was never my intention to hurt her. We didn't speak for much longer. The conversation ended when she said she hated me and hung up.

What had I done? I felt so bad. I went into the living room. I was crying, surrounded by all this pain and I was the creator of it. As I lay down on the chair I said to myself, *I deserve this.* I was thinking about Kim, asking God for help yet again asking my Angels could they please go to Kim at this time as I did not need them. I put my hands on my heart, it was like I was asking everyone for their help. I felt really tired all of a sudden. I was asking my Guide, Danny for some help. I asked him to let me see him. *Please Danny I really need you.* I drifted off to sleep. I am not sure for how long but when I started to wake up I could feel something at my feet. You know when you're half awake, your eyes are trying to focus, it's like coming from a dark room into light. Well that's the way it was for me.

I felt the energy at my feet. I opened my eyes fully. There he was, Danny my Spirit Guide, standing at the end of the chair. He manifested to me from Spirit. Danny was really tall, about 6ft 2ins. He was wearing brown desert boots, blue jeans and a checked red and black shirt. He had a beard. He looked around mid to late 40's. I got a little fright as you would expect! I jumped, closed my eyes and when I opened them he had disappeared. I started asking questions, *why did he disappear*? He told me he was by my side for the phone call. His message was that everything happens for a reason.

"Don't beat yourself up. We are all on a journey. You were ready to see me. I manifested to validate that everything is happening perfectly. I am telling you that you will get the chance to make peace with Kim but she needs time to be angry and heal. When you asked your Angels to help they heard that—they have surrounded Kim with love and light."

I could see the light of my uncle and aunt's car pulling in and with that my communication ended. The kids were hyper. I was being my usual playful self and the kids were getting even more hyper! Tammy asked was I okay? "You look like you have been crying."

"I am fine," I lied. I waited until later that evening when everyone was gone to bed except Brian and I. I told him I spoke with Kim and it wasn't a nice conversation but I did feel better. I didn't say how the phone call happened or about Danny my Spirit Guide manifesting to me. My uncle being the wise old soul always seemed to have the right answers and could put things into perspective all the time, even from the worst situation he always saw the light. This was a great quality of his and one he was teaching me. I was so grateful.

I just prayed to God that night, asking that all would be okay. I asked God to never leave me and that I wanted to live to the best of my ability.

I was having really vivid dreams. A lot of the time I would come out of my body and fly to places in my dream state. I was going to spiritual school in a dream state. I would wake up the next day with new knowledge or there would be a shift in my consciousness. My understanding was opening up to love, compassion and forgiveness. I was slowly learning to forgive myself and see how I treated my own thoughts and feelings.

I dreamt I saw my grandfather. He was showing me how happy he was and all the good work he was doing. Then he brought me to my mother and father, showing me the love they had for me and the love I had for them. The message he brought to me was: "it's easier in life to point the finger than accept the change. Everything will change when you change. This is the only answer." What he also showed me that night was to look as some photos, which were taken at Niagara Falls and my apartment when I first arrived in America. In the dream it was showing me that I had something to see in them.

When I woke the next morning I searched for the pictures. I pulled my room apart and when I finally found them I noticed there were a few pictures with same smokey image. I looked at them all day. I knew this was my Spirit Guide, Danny. There was also Angel energy in the photos. There were orbs in the pictures too. Yet again, this was another validation that I was on the right path. They were telling me to trust, they have always been around me.

I brought the photos up to ask Brian and Tammy to take a look. Their thoughts were the same as mine. I had looked at these pictures loads of times before, I had never seen these signs until now. *How come I can see them now?*

"We are always here for all to see, but most people's vibration is not tuned into that, so as you went through your clearing things became clearer."

What I thought was even more crazy was that some of the photos were taken when I first arrived in America, well over a year and a half ago and they were taken on a disposable camera!

Lots of people said things like that could only be captured on digital camera, but here I was been given evidence at every opportunity! It was time for me to put my faith into action, get out of the left-brain and stop looking for logical answers all of the time! It was time for me to explore the creative side of the brain, the side with no limitations. I was being given hard evidence and proof of my life. What was really shining through for me was that I was part of a bigger picture, a plan, and I was beginning to see this. We were going to the Medium's home that Sunday so I said I would bring the photos to see what he could tell me.

Circle ? What is That?

It was Sunday morning. I was up bright and early feeling very excited about going to this spiritual circle. I asked Brian to explain to me exactly what a circle was. I thought everyone went there and sat around in a circle! He laughed and said "kind of, but at this meeting we will be sitting in rows." I asked him what I should expect. "Who will be there?" I asked. "All kinds of people. There will be healers, people who work with crystals, people who work with Angels and Spirit," he replied. I laughed thinking *Oh my god I am going to some hippy commune!*

I had been for a palm and tealeaf reading before but not like this. I put my coin into a special little holder and packed my photos. The whole way there all I thought about was my Grandfather. I wondered if he would bring me a message. I knew my uncle Brian wanted a message. Brian wanted to make contact so I was wishing my Granddad to come to him. I had no communications with my own Angels and Guide, it was like it was their day off! I laughed to myself.

The Medium lived about twenty minutes away. My hands were a little sweaty and my heartbeat was a little faster than normal. I asked Brian and Tammy how long it would go on for. They told me it would be a couple of hours. This was all very exciting, but as we pulled up at the house something came over me. I became the biggest sceptic ever! I didn't say anything to my uncle or aunt.

As we pulled into the drive there were lots of people standing outside the Medium's house. I think I was the youngest there! Tammy and Brian started chatting to some people outside. I was checking the place out. I got chatting to a few people. They had nothing but praise for this guy and had the nicest things to say. He sounded like a truly amazing guy. I was curious to see what everyone else was going on about. There was a porch to the side of his home, I was standing inside waiting to go in. Tammy and Brian instructed me to take off my shoes. I was thinking there would be a smell of feet inside! *Why do we have to take off our shoes? Have I any holes in the toes of my socks?* Being a little sceptical of this guy I thought that he had listening devices outside and inside the room, that he would listen to what people said before the group started and then come in and make a connection!

I decided to sit at the very back of the room. Brian and Tammy sat at the front. I had my arms folded guarding myself, scanning the room to see if he had planted stuff to hear what was going on!

Well, let me tell you I was in for a shock this day, it was another part of the puzzle. The circle was about to start. There was silence and in comes the Medium. He wasn't what I had imagined in my mind. He introduced himself and gave us an introduction to what was going to be covered in the class. I was listening, trying to fight my scepticism. He asked us to pack away the chairs and lie on the floor. There were window seats, some people sat on them as there wasn't enough room on the floor for everyone. His space was lovely, all wooden, white and cream. He also had lots of crystals which I had never seen before. Some of them were really big, they were beautiful.

He instructed us to lay our hand on the person next to us and to get a blanket if we needed one. I wasn't feeling anything in the room. My guys definitely took the morning off! He asked us to close our eyes and focus on our breathing which I was already doing. Then he asked us to imagine this golden white light around us. He started bringing us through a guided meditation. This was my first ever-guided meditation. I was struggling and I found it hard for my mind to relax. I was moving around on the floor, my legs twitching. *This is a load of crap.* Everyone else seemed to just get right into it but here's the Irish boy moving around the floor like Michael Flatley in Lord of the Dance! The Medium was still talking away. He was bringing us down a flight of stairs counting the steps. I couldn't see them let alone count them! Then I felt these hands on my head and his voice next to me. He had put his hands on my head, there was lots of pressure and heat, just like the heat I felt when I laid my hands on my body. I could feel myself getting very relaxed. I was going deeper and deeper. My mind wasn't racing. All the thoughts slipped away. I got to the bottom of the stairs and I saw this massive symbol. It was like two snakes intertwined going up a sword. I could still feel these hands on my head, only now I could hear his voice at the other side of the room. *Who had their hands on my head?* He brought us back up the stairs and back into the room.

The second I opened my eyes I looked around the room—no-one had their hands on my head. I looked at the Medium. People were asking lots of questions. I probably had a stunned look on my face. "What did you see?" he asked me.

"I saw these two snakes, they looked like they were attached to this sword with wings. I have never seen this before," I replied.

"This is the holy snake you have seen. It is very powerful. It is a symbol, your Kundalini, which is the movement of energy. It is for healing and it unites fear and hope, surrender and courage. He turned away and started answering other questions. I was thinking *fear is something I have lots of, hope is my message from my Guardian Angel, and healing is what my Angel said I was—a healer.* It was like another small piece to the jigsaw.

He spoke for a short while after this about things that were going on at the present time. Then he took a break. He asked if anyone wanted healing but for some strange reason a group of people had taken Brian outside. He was lying on the ground with these big crystals all over his body and lots of people around him. They were giving him a group healing, it looked amazing. I was deep in thought, having lots of resistance, but wanting to break free. I was around these people for a reason. Brian was still on the floor. It looked like he was releasing loads of stuff as people were laying their hands on him and chanting things, it was some experience to look at. I was thinking in the back of my mind *what if they could all see me at home at this, what would they say?* The break was over and we made our way back into the room. It was full of energy, very warm and the energy felt amazing. The Medium came back and started talking. It sounded like he was giving a message from Spirit. People were asking him lots of questions. He worked his way around the room—I was at the back of the room—right at the back wall—if I got any further I would have been in the garden! The next thing he was standing right in front me! He said "you're not from here, are you?" *That wouldn't be hard ... I am the only one in the room with a strong Irish accent! The only other Irish person is my uncle but his accent has an American twang to it*. He continued, "I mean you're not from America." I didn't reply. "You come from a small town ... it's Drog ... he said its Drog ... I can't say it!" I knew why he couldn't say the name, it's a name that most people wouldn't be used to seeing or saying unless you were from Ireland. Guess what? He was right! My hometown is called Drogheda! He had my attention now. The scepticism was not long disappearing.

 "I have a man here and he wants to bring you a message. I feel he's like your grandfather. Does the initial P mean anything? *Yes* I think. "Hold on, his name is Paddy." Well this is my grandfather's name—he had me hook, line and sinker! "He also wants to call you this— 'mickser'. Well if this was a message from my grandfather it was so accurate. I came from a massive family. On my mother's side there were 14 brothers and sisters so you can imagine how many grandchildren there was. The word 'mickser' was my grandfather's special nickname for us. I had just received a massive healing. The man loved by us all was right there. I couldn't see my granddad but I felt him and his energy as the space around us got colder. "He also wants to say he has a dog here with him. The dog loves rocks or stones and hasn't a tooth in his head! Hold on, Bruce do you know this name?" "Yes, that was our dog," I replied. "We grew up with him as children. He hadn't a tooth in his head!" There was also more meaning for me. Bruce got poisoned. When he was dying I spent a day trying to get him to eat and drink before he died. I felt sad inside. The Medium continued "He wants you to know that Bruce still comes to you and watches over you." I was so happy hearing this. He then mentioned my mother and about us not speaking. "You need to contact her." I nodded knowing exactly what he meant. "Your grandfather loves you dearly, but you will connect with him in more ways than one from today, so be ready! And with that the communication ended. I was so happy inside. *What more could I have asked for*. I didn't mention my coin. I never took it out to show anyone. I didn't get to show him the photos, but I knew the time wasn't right.

 The circle was coming to an end. A lady introduced herself to me by the name of Paula. She was a real stunning lady. The energy coming from her was so soft and gentle. She was lovely. "I am a Reiki master. Why don't you and your uncle come for some healing?" she asked.

This would be the first time I had ever heard of Reiki or Reiki Master. I was buzzing. I said I would love to go so we exchanged numbers and agreed to meet.

I thought to myself *Master—is this what my Guardian Angel meant?* The universe was starting to open my path, sending the people I needed to me. I made some other friends that day too. I left no longer the sceptic. My foundation was truly set. This Medium was the most honest and genuine guy I had ever met. No ego. This guy came from the heart and was truly gifted. In my eyes he was an Earth Angel helping so many souls.

We left for home. I don't think my bum touched the seat the whole way home—I was so high on life! I thanked my grandfather for coming. I thought *I will phone mom when I get home.* There was a silence on the way home. We were all deep in thought. Our faces alight with the light of God within us and life kept on saying it had meaning.

We arrived back and I phoned home. My brother Joe answered. This would be my first challenge, small but still a challenge. Brian and Tammy had been chatting to people at home and must have said 'you won't know Robbie when you see him, he's a changed man.' Well they took this up in a different way! My brother Joe is the biggest joker ever. He started taking the piss out of me saying "I hear you are all holy now! You're going to mass and everything—you have been converted!" I took the defence a little and said to him, "you wouldn't understand." "Sure I would, you are a bible basher now," he joked. "Do you believe in God, Joe?" I asked. "Yeah, he replied. "Well why do you mock God?" I asked. There was silence. He didn't know what to say back to that. I loved my brother so much but it was the only answer that came to mind. I really felt empowered and for the first time ever, I acknowledged myself and the part of God that lives within me. I never said it to hurt him nor did he say what he said to hurt me.

My mom came on the phone. I told her that I had been to see this Medium and granddad was there.

"What do you mean? Granddad is dead," mom said.

"No he is not—he lives in spirit and through this guy today he brought me this message. He told me lots of things but most of all he said that we should speak. I'm sorry. I love you." This was one of the most difficult things I had ever done. Things were back on track.

(Song—*This Little Light of Mine* Harry Dixon Loes— Gospel Version)

There will be times when you will feel like you're on your knees, when all HOPE seems to be fading away. If you have ever gone into a room and it is in complete darkness, and you light a candle, the candle will light up the room. There will always be shadows where the light reflects off things in the room, but with the candle light, the darkness cannot quench the light. The darkness will never dampen out the brightness of the light. The only way the darkness will ever go is if it turns into light. Life will bring us only what we can handle, nothing more, nothing less. Our family, friends and relationships in this life are so complex, yet so easy. When we learn to come from a place of love, this will be when we most shine bright and our light will be like the lighthouse guiding the ships from a stormy sea. Always remember that the light from the lighthouse will shine but it cannot stop ships from crashing onto rocks or running a ground. So love many, forgive even more, for the eyes of HOPE are shining on you once more.

We all sat around the table that night chatting about the day. My uncle was so happy for me. He could see me changing. My light was starting to shine again. I was on cloud nine. I was happy that I had spoken to my mom. For the first time in my whole life I had my faith, it was unbreakable. I knew God was real. I knew my life was real. I had this feeling of fullness within me. When I looked at my Uncle Brian and Aunt Tammy, their eyes said the same.

Brian and I were excited about going to see Paula for some Reiki healing. There was something more to this lady. She had a presence about her, this sense of purity. We were so blessed to have met her.

I was seeing lots of number sequences at this time on cloaks, the TV, number plates, for example 4:44 5:55 9:11 or 11:11. I felt very drawn to numbers. Brian had a book on numerology. We took it out and looked at what the numbers meant. I noticed when my Angel or Spirit Guide would come, these numbers would flash on the clock so it was all part of my awakening. These were more signs from the other side saying they are here and the number sequences were the confirmation. This book showed you how to find your life path number by adding up your date of birth, so for mine it was 3rd August 1978, which in numerology is the number 9. To get this life path number you simply add up your date of birth, for example, $3 + 8 + 1 + 9 + 7 + 8 = 36 = 3 + 6 = 9$.

The book also gave you a colour for your life path number and its meaning. I added mine just like above, which was very interesting. I also added my families. A life path number could tell a lot about a person and their character. I had a deep passion for these numbers and the understanding these could bring into peoples' lives.

Brian and I were messing around with the tarot cards as we spoke more about our recent Medium experience.

Brian said "I told you the Medium was good."

I asked him "Do you think this is what I will do?" Even though after seeing the Medium that day I really could see now what I was going to do, I still wasn't exactly sure as to how I was going to get there. Even though my Guardian Angel told me my path, it was like I was still seeking a further guidance or reassurance from Brian.

"Yes Robbie, you will work with people and help them. You have a great journey ahead of you," he affirmed.

I was telling Brian that when I lay in bed at night I would receive information like I was plugged into the world-wide-web. Anything I looked for in my mind would be there! I was trying to explain this. I knew he understood, but sometimes when someone else is explaining their experience it can be very hard for us to fully understand if we are not experiencing the same things. I explained it the best way I could.

We would set each other little challenges each night. This evening we got the whole tarot deck and placed them face down on the table. We would see who could pick a card, for example, Brian would point at a card and say "what is that one?" I would say "Four of Wands" and we would turn it over. If it were the Four of Wands you would take another turn. Brian picked and I went first. "What's this one Robbie?"

Out of my mouth came the words "6 of Cups." He turned it over and
I got it right! And the next one—the 2 of Wands, right again! And the
next one, the 6 of Swords. The look on Brian's face was priceless! *How
the hell am I doing this?* We kept on going. The only way I can explain
what was happening here was, when Brian would ask me to guess the
cards, a really strong feeling would come over me and out of my mouth
would come the name of the card.

That night I guessed every single card in the deck, except two. I
couldn't believe it. I would say my intuition at this time was most pure
as I had no other influence from the outside world, it was a straight
connection back to my higher self. It was like the child that comes
into the world with his or her gifts and everything flows freely with
no fear or judgement. It wasn't that I was special. This was coming
from a place of complete trust just like all the gifts that's with each and
everyone of us. I was lucky to be in a place where I was surrounded by
love to be able to nurture the natural side of my ability, connect to my
higher self and God. I was so excited and grateful at this time in my
life. Yes, I felt different to others. I was starting to understand a little
bit about myself, still some of the answers for this would come from
my childhood, through my teens to an adult. The answers were making
their way towards me.

As my Guardian Angel told me 'there is not one more soul here
that is more gifted than another.' I was starting to feel this and know
my job would be to show others the way through light. I was also
thinking about my healing. I received the symbol, The Holy Snake and
the meaning of this which meant uniting fear and hope. This brought
me back to the question, *what did she mean when see brought me the
message of HOPE?* I was looking for the answer because this was the
key to my path in life.

I went to bed that night and asked my Guardian Angel for the
answer. *What does HOPE mean? Please tell me!* I was also asking my
Spirit Guide, Danny. I didn't hear anything from Danny so I started
writing in my diary. The answers still did not come. It was like the
silence had arrived again only this time I understood it. I didn't jump
into a place of fear or think they had left. I just accepted that they never

leave us—that they cannot bring us every single answer or do this 24/7, it is not the will of God. We as humans have to live out our own experiences to learn. If I was caught up in their reality all the time I would be missing out on the one biggest GIFT I had been given—the gift of LIFE! I expected answers there and then and when the answers didn't come directly, I had no choice but to wait and learn that it would come in the universe's time divinely guided. I was beginning to learn the art of patience.

16

Healing Hands: Its What's in your Heart

Brian and I contacted Paula to arrange for our Reiki healing. I was really looking forward to it. It felt like such a treat to be around other like-minded people. We had booked our session for Tuesday evening. I asked Brian "what's this Reiki thing?" "What do they do?" He explained that Reiki healers put their hands on or off your body channelling universal light of unconditional love from God which helps people to self-heal." I was very excited. I knew Paula had a really strong and special energy. I was wondering whether I would tell Paula about my coin and my Guardian Angel. I wasn't sure so I decided to just 'go with the flow.' I was still in full conversation with God, my Guardian Angel and Spirit Guide even if the answers weren't been given, I still asked. *HOPE, what is the meaning?*

It was time for us to make our way to Paula's house. It was 5:55. Everything is happening perfectly en route, we are both chatting not knowing what to expect. We arrived and rang the doorbell. As Paula answered the door I saw these massive rays of light behind her, it was nearly blinding me! I never said anything. There were lots of Angels around her, the energy in her home was amazing. I felt an instant connection to her. When I looked into her eyes I felt like I knew her, I could see her soul or what I would learn to say further down the line, her light.

She offered us some tea and we both took herbal tea. She then asked who wanted to go first. Brian went first for his Reiki treatment whilst I waited in her living room. All the time I was in the living room the room was full of Angels. I could see their light. I felt the energy shifting in the home which was an amazing experience.

When Brian's healing was finished he looked different, like he was floating, super relaxed. I was still contemplating telling her about my coin. Paula brought me into her healing room. It was beautiful. Everything had its perfect place. She started explaining what Reiki healing was and how it would work for me. She asked if I ever had a healing before. I was just about to say no when I remembered my neighbour who gave me a massage before going to America and the heat from her hands. I decided not to say I was laying my hands on myself feeling massive waves of heat. She explained that she would put her hands on different points of my body called chakras. Each chakra had a different colour and meaning. I nodded. I knew about chakras but I wasn't a Master on them. Paula had a special bed called a plinth. I lay down and she put a blanket over me. I closed my eyes and I started to drift off. I could feel the heat from Paula's hands. Holy moly, it was like I was sitting on the beach at mid-day! I had my eyes closed. It felt like I had this pressure all over me my head. It started to feel like it was going to explode! Then I experienced this massive release, my whole body tingled. She started to speak to me, "Robbie, you are very special. You have come here to help people. You have many angels with you. You also see Angels and have done since a child. Your vision will become clearer. You saw lots of light when you came here today. This is the light of the Archangel Gabriel and Michael. These are just some of the Angels you will see and work with, but you also work with Spirit realms, it will be this work that will start you off. What I have to tell you is that you have healing hands and when the time is right you will use them". I was in a place of pure bliss. I drifted further and further, and deeper and deeper. I heard her voice call me "it's time to come back into the room." I started to wake up or come back. I could see her standing about 2ft away yet I could feel her hands on me! She smiled. "There were many angels here tonight," Paula shared. Now I know why Brian looked like he was floating—I was now floating too! She warned me to me be careful that I could come out of my body quite easily. She advised me to remember to always ground myself like the roots of a sycamore tree. I understood a bit but not fully.

We went back out into the living room. Paula asked what I thought of the Medium. "Amazing," I replied. "He is an Earth Angel." In the back of my mind I was thinking, *I have met another one tonight! God has placed you in my life for a reason.* Brian and I said it was a pity there wouldn't be another meeting for a month. Paula informed us that there would be one this weekend because he had plans and had to move it forward. I was delighted. Brian and I confirmed we would definitely be there. We went to pay her for our healing but she wouldn't accept the money. "This is my gift to you. Remember you have healing hands." I couldn't thank her enough, such kindness. What a star she was. "Thank you Paula, you have helped me so much," I said. As I made my way to the car I looked back and she was standing at the door surrounded by this beautiful prism of light. I thought to myself, *I have seen this light before.*

I knew I wanted to go for another healing. It was amazing. I had experienced this deep awakening. I knew one day I was going to work with people like Paula. It was like the universe was presenting to me the things I needed to see, in order to find myself and my path.

Brian and I felt really good. I spoke to Brian about Kim on the way home. I didn't know what to do even though our relationship was over we had not verbalised this. I really wanted to say sorry. I never meant to hurt her.

I was feeling like I had found the one true place of happiness. I felt this was the place I wanted to settle. I loved being around Brian and Tammy, they were amazing people. I was thinking about looking for an apartment. However, there were still obstacles to overcome. I was still an illegal alien so that meant I couldn't drive and that was a big challenge. It meant if anyone was sick at home or was getting married I couldn't go home or I wouldn't get back into America. I really felt this was my home. I loved the people. I loved the country. There was so much choice. I loved the weather—experiencing four proper seasons was amazing. I asked Brian for advice—he always had the right answers! He thought I should phone Kim again and try to make things right as it would help me grow. He also said I could stay with them for as long as I wanted to, there was no rush to get my own place. I knew he meant this from the heart but I still felt I needed to maybe give them some space. So I planned to stay in America illegally, hoping something would come up that would give me the opportunity to become legal. I started to ask my Angels and Spirit Guide Danny for help with this. I also asked for help with Kim.

Stay or Go? Boom or Bust?

Christmas was round the corner and I was making a plan to stay. Brian's business was a little slower than normal. I knew he was under a little pressure but he didn't tell me much. I knew things were tight financially. He was talking about the 'boom' that was happening back in Ireland, the Celtic tiger it was known as, it appeared like the whole country was working. There were lots of big jobs. Brian went on to tell me about his reading with the Medium. The message my grandfather had brought him was that he would go back to Ireland. He didn't think this was going to happen nor did I. There was too much here for him to pack up and go back home to Ireland. He had been in the states for twenty years. I felt it was his way of getting some stress off his chest. I didn't think for one minute that he was really considering going home.

Brian was selling some cars at the time. He had a friend who came in and fix them up and he would sell them. This guy was very nice, a decent, honest guy. He said he was a mechanic, but there was no way he was because anything he seemed to fix would only get to the front gate of my uncle's place and break down! He was costing him more money and putting him under a lot of pressure. He would just take tools out and they would go missing. I went into the garage, tidy up and put all the tools back into their boxes. But this was a complete waste of time because he would come behind you and leave all the stuff lying around. My uncle Brian was a real kind person, a good Samaritan. He knew this guy needed the money so he helped him out but the consequence was his pocket was getting emptier. This was the first time I saw my uncle stressed. I was worried about him. I was also really thinking about myself and my own future. I didn't want to go back home to Ireland. I didn't know how I would cope. *Would I be back to the partying and taking drugs? Would I walk in those old shoes again? Would I get away from the person everyone feels they know? I am not the guy who got on the plane to come here. If I have to go back will it still be the same people doing the same things, drinking in bars telling the same old stories?* Even though there was no decision to go home from my uncle, it definitely got me thinking.

17

Validation and Synchronicities at Their Best

It was the morning of the next meeting at the Medium's. We were all excited. Tammy had arranged a babysitter so we could all go. I felt really giddy. We waited for the babysitter to come. She was running late. I started to think she wasn't coming. I asked Brian to give her a call as we didn't want to be late. He tried to ring her but got no answer. He tried again—still no answer. Time was ticking by. Brian said to go ahead and when the babysitter arrived he would follow. We all stood in the house each one of us saying, "no you go, I will stay." Because I couldn't drive Brian told me and Tammy to go ahead and he would follow us. I asked the Angels to get us there in time. I had my coin and my photos with me. The only person who knew about that day was Tammy.

The place was packed. I took off my shoes in the porch and noticed the change in the weather, it had gotten dull. I saw Paula and a few other faces from the last time. I made my way to the back of the room, it was nearly the same seat that I had sat in before. I sat beside a girl who sat to the right of me. She had blonde hair and was a pretty girl with a soft energy. I was there this time as a believer, viewing this from a whole different space. I felt great. Tammy sat up near the front of the room. We waited for the Medium to come and start. I had my coin in my pocket. I decided to take it out and hold it in my hand, my left hand. I gripped it really tight, not letting anyone see it. I looked around the room sensing the different energies from different people but not seeing any light around them. There was a silence in the room. As the clouds outside changed so did the light in the room. The Medium appeared and began the class. He started with a different meditation this time. I felt really relaxed. I felt some sort of connection to the girl sitting next to me but I was unsure what it was. The meditation finished, I felt really clear in my mind, at ease. The Medium talked about some planetary stuff and things that were shifting. There were people putting their hands up and asking questions.

I am still holding my coin not letting anyone see it. I could feel my special connection to the coin. He would answer people's questions, making his way around the room being guided towards different people. Then he made his way to the back of the room and stood right in front of me. He looked at me really funny. I was sweating, my hands felt clammy. I was shaking a little and I felt my body temperature change. "You met her, didn't you?" he said to me. I looked at him nodding my head. He says it again, "You met her. YOU MET YOUR GUARDIAN ANGEL. SHE CAME TO YOU, DIDN'T SHE?" She crossed over to you and met you physically. "Yes", I was nodding as I filled with excitement and shock. *Oh my God, he knows! I am getting the biggest validation ever!* Now everyone in the room is looking at me, my face has turned bright red. "She gave you something, didn't she? Open your hand, please," he said. I opened my hand and his face light up. This glow came from him. My hand was opened with my coin in it. "Your Guardian Angel came to you with this coin as a sign. May I hold it, please?" he asks. "Of course," I replied. What I remember most was the silence in the room. He took the coin and lifted it up, turned it around so everyone else in the room could see the special coin. He continued "If I was to put every single person in this room together as one you would not have as much faith as that one young man." I have to be really honest when I heard these words, I sat back in my chair and looked over my shoulder thinking *he must be talking about some else, that's not me!* I remember thinking to myself *if he had a clue what I have done in my past he would not say that.* But that was all my own insecurities.

"You met your Guardian Angel. She gave you your coin of HOPE & FAITH."

I was really taken aback and still blushing yet I had the biggest smile on my face EVER! It was all part of the transformation. He gave me back the coin and said, "You must keep that coin close to you at all times." Off he went to the next person.

The girl sitting next to me asked could she see the coin and hold it. I asked her name, she said it was Sue-Ellen. I introduced myself and gave her my coin. As she held the coin she told me that she had dreamt about me the night before and had seen my coin in the dream. After she woke up out of the dream she felt like she had to write a poem. "I have it here." I couldn't believe it!

What the hell is going on? It seems to be one thing after another. Yet another synchronicity—showing me my life had meaning and depth. Sue-Ellen took out the poem she had written from her dream. I opened it. This is what it said:

> A cross in his palm, his hands so strong.
> The cross reminds me of the crosses I bear.
> It is his faith, his luck? I want to touch it.
> Will I feel the strength from it that he does? I want to touch his hand.
> He holds it so tight in his fist. This tells me he believes in it.
> He believes in having something to hold and believe his special gift,
> his coin.

You can imagine how I was feeling after reading this poem and the Medium validating my Guarding Angel, and then my coin, he even knew I had it in my hand! When he spoke about faith I thought *who me? Surely not me! What does he mean?* Then I sat beside a girl that had a dream about me and wrote a poem about the coin sent from the heavens!

> Life has a plan and it's our choice to be awake
> or sleeping along the path.
> Thy will, not their will.

The circle finished that afternoon. Tammy and I were chatting, we were in total amazement still. She was so supportive, I was so happy that she was there for the experience. Brian never made it because the babysitter didn't show. I really wished he had been there, I couldn't wait to tell him what had happened.

We were chatting to different people and I got chatting to Paula. I was so delighted to see her. Some people wanted to see the coin, this would be the start of a long journey of people seeing and holding the special coin. I was telling Paula a little about how I received my coin and we arranged to meet again this time at Brian and Tammy's.

I got an opportunity to show the Medium my photos. He confirmed what I had felt—It was my Spirit Guide and orbs in the photos. I really wanted to go to him for a reading as I felt it would be of great benefit. I asked if he had any appointments, he said that he had nothing available until the end of January or February but he wouldn't know until he saw his diary. I agreed to call him to check his availability and I thanked him for my message.

It was nearly time for Tammy and I to go home. Sue-Ellen was outside. We exchanged numbers and agreed to keep in touch. I was so grateful for the poem. I knew I would meet her again soon.

I didn't stop talking the whole way home. It was lovely to spend some time with Tammy. She had a great sense of humour and a great way of bringing the funny side out in me. So the whole way home she would crack jokes and do silly things. My sides would need stitching up after because I laughed that much. When the Medium gave me the validation about my Guardian Angel, the feelings that ran through my body were surreal. It was like being on the highest high on drugs but without the drugs! *So what was life showing me at this time? That you can have these euphoric moments and be in a place of complete bliss, high on life, without any external influence or substance! That it can all come from within and this is not something that is just gifted to one person, it is there for us all!*

We arrived back at the house buzzing—high on life! Brian was a little quieter than usual. I knew he really wanted to be there. I felt bad that he missed out as we shared our experiences. I told him about Sue-Ellen and how she had a dream with me in it, my coin and that she had wrote a poem about them. I didn't want to go on too much, as I knew he was a little pissed off because the babysitter didn't show up.

I met up with Sue-Ellen a couple of times. It was great because she was also young and on her own spiritual journey, so we had lots in common. It was great to talk about Angels, Spirits and healing. I was learning a lot from her. Like me, she had her own spiritual perils along her journey to awakening. She had two wonderful children and as a single mother she was doing a really good job.

You Better Get Home Here Quick. What Goes Up Surely Must Come Down!

It was getting close to Christmas and I was helping my uncle in his garage. We had to go to the army barracks to drop off some starters and alternators for some army vehicles he was working on. My uncle had taking in this pickup truck for a service with a few other little jobs. It was a Ford F350. He got his buddy the mechanic to do the job. Now let me explain, Brian's home had a fully working garage which was connected to his home, so you could walk from the house into a little office and straight onto the garage floor. There was a four-poster lift, big enough to fit a limousine on. It was an automated lift so you could raise the vehicle safely from the ground from a start button. There was a safety mechanism on it so that at each level it went to these safety pins would click in. You had to listen for them. Once you heard all four clicks it was then safe to let it back down.

So we are out on this delivery. I will never forget this day. The weather was horrible. It looked like the sky was about to fall out of the heavens. As we drove to the army barracks Brian noticed he was low on fuel so we started looking for a garage. Before we left, Brian had warned the mechanic to be careful with the lift as the pickup truck was big and heavy. This guy had a habit of half doing things! Brian's phone rang a couple times but he was under a lot pressure to get the job to the army barracks so he never answered it. We came across a petrol station, filled up the tank and made our way to the barracks just in the nick of time. Brian said to me that he had this really bad feeling that something was not right. With that the phone rang again. It was Tammy.

There had been an accident at Brian and Tammy's, we raced home. We arrived at the house and drove around to the back, the garage door was opened fully. I saw the mechanic standing there and he was as white as a sheet smoking a cigarette like it was the last one he would ever smoke! For a split second we thought Tammy was messing. Then we pulled into full view and saw the pickup truck had run off the lift and through the wall into the office! Brian was in complete silence, I had never seen a man so quiet in my life. The mechanic raced over to the window saying, "I am sorry. I don't know what happened." In the calmest voice ever Brian says, "Are you okay?" as he looks at this big pickup truck smashed through the wall of the house. "What happened?" Brian asked. "I had the lift up full and went to put it down—three pins stayed locked and the front gave way." Brian and I knew this wasn't true as he had put the lift up fully but never listened to see if the four pins locked and then let the lift down hence the pickup truck came crashing off the lift! What was even scarier was the kids would often come from the house to the garage if we were there. Tammy confirmed that the kids were out there only two minutes before it happened. They were so lucky. Tammy said she was out by the lift and next thing was she had this strong urge to go inside with the kids. When she went inside she heard the crash. I knew that this was the Angels helping and Tammy listening to her gut feeling and trusting. Brian was still in silence apart from making sure everyone was okay. He asked me to make sure everything was switched off and the doors were locked. He said he would be in in a minute. He paid the mechanic and sent him on his way, turned off the rest of the lights and went into the house.

Everyone was safe. There was nothing we could do about the vehicle in his office. It was all really serious yet I really felt like laughing. Have you ever been in that situation where you really don't want to laugh but you can't help it? Brian came in, put the TV on and never said a word. I couldn't look at him because I thought I was going to laugh. Tammy couldn't look at me because she's the same—holding in the laughter. There is a silence and out of nowhere Brian lets this massive scream! He is going mad, screaming his head off. This just completely sets me off laughing. Brian is screaming, "There is a three and half ton pickup in my f***ing office which belongs to a f***ing costumer!" I can't help but laugh at him screaming his head off.

Tammy starts laughing, then the kids joined in and before we know it we're all laughing. If anyone could have seen us! From pain to laughter! Brian went from 'what am I going to do?' to 'f*** it, sure it's a wonderful surprise right before Christmas!'

This was the final nail in the coffin. It was the day that Brian decided to go back to Ireland. I wasn't prepared for this. I had now set my heart on staying in America. We locked the doors that day and just said 'f*** it.' It was out of our hands. There was nothing that we could have changed in the moment.

At breakfast the next morning Brian said he was really thinking of moving back home. There was so much work in Ireland at that time. I knew his business was sinking him so it was the best decision for him and his family. But it totally turned my plans upside down. I didn't know what to do, I was in limbo. I needed to make a decision and I hadn't got long. Brian told me I could stay on and live with Tammy's parents. It was a great offer but my heart was saying no. I was fearful about going home. Would people understand me now? I was on this spiritual path, not smoking or drinking and communicating with my Angels and Spirit family again. I really felt that there were lots of closed minds at home and there were big challenges ahead for me.

It was Christmas and we were all in high spirits. Brian and Tammy were excited about their new life in Ireland. I was just living in the moment. I tried to call Kim over the Christmas but we never got to speak. I still wanted to make peace for everything she helped me with. I also wanted to tell her that I was going back home to Ireland.

I was hanging out with Sue-Ellen a lot. Our friendship developed into a romantic relationship. We had lots of things in common and had this crazy spiritual connection. This was the first time ever in my life I would experience this.

I was starting to think about what my life would be like back in Ireland. I called my best buddy Neala to tell her the news. She asked me to come back to New York that she would find me some work that I could move back in with her, but I just couldn't do it. I didn't feel I was strong enough to live or work in the city. I still had pain from the accident on the fourth of July. Living illegally wasn't something

I wanted. Living with Brian and Tammy had lots of safety but going back to the city I would be watching over my shoulder. I just couldn't do it. Neala totally understood and wished me well.

It was also time to let the others at home know that my American dream was coming to an end. I would probably have to move back to my parent's house. This would be tough, but sure I wouldn't stay for long, I thought.

I called home to tell my family the good news. I would be coming home at the end of January 2003. I spoke with mom and I asked her if I could move back in with them when I came home for a short while. She was happy and asked if I would be home for my sisters 21st birthday. I could surprise her. I was excited about this and was looking forward to seeing her. I was also excited about seeing my little brother Jason who I knew wasn't so little anymore from what my mom was saying. It sounded like he had grown up overnight. I was looking forward to seeing my whole family. *Would my family know me?* I was not the person who left Ireland back in 2001.

I had been also asking mom about my best friend Lee and how was he doing. Mom said he was not too good. He had been in some trouble and didn't think things were going good. I was worried about him. Lee was like a son to my parents.

I was doing lots of writing at this point, asking my Angels for as much guidance as I could get, asking them, *why am I going back to Ireland when my heart belonged in America?* I was having lots of conversations in my mind. I didn't always get the direct answer but their presence was always there. I still believe it was the never-ending conversations that made me stronger. They also helped make the connection stronger.

We passed through Christmas and into the New Year. It was January and the clock was ticking. Brian and Tammy had lots to do. They were selling their belongings and packing up stuff. I wasn't working at the time and I hadn't much cash so they kindly paid for my ticket home. I was nervous about flying home thinking *what if I get stopped leaving the country and pulled in for being illegal?* It would be a five or ten year ban if I got caught. *Would I ever be able to come back?*

18

A Visitor With a Difference

Brian and Tammy would very rarely lie in, but if they did I would go in and chat to them in their bedroom. Our conversations would always be about Angels and Spirit and it was great to listen to both their wisdom.

We were chatting one morning about different things, mostly about going back home to Ireland. They were now starting to think that this was the best decision for them. It was hard for them. It was such a big move to find new jobs, schools for the kids and a new home.

They had a small TV in their bedroom. It was on in the background and we were chatting away. I was lying at the bottom of their bed and the TV switched off. We didn't pay any attention and continued chatting away. The TV came back on and then off again. "Okay, stop messing. Who has the remote control?" Brian asked. I looked at Tammy because she is the joker. Brian looked at Tammy, "You have them, don't you, Tammy?" "No, I haven't. You have them, Robbie?" "No, I don't," I replied. The TV is back on now. "Come on, you have them!" Tammy and I said to Brian. "No, I haven't!" he exclaimed. We started laughing! Tammy looked around and noticed the remote control sitting at the side of the TV. "Look, it's over there," Tammy pointed. We all looked at each other, our faces alight. Brian asked "If there is someone else from the Spirit world in this room then turn the volume up." He no more had the words out when the TV went onto full volume. It was so loud. Brian then asked if the volume could go down. Sure enough, the volume started to go down. We looked at each other in amazement. The hairs were standing on the back of our neck and arms! We still looked at each other to see if there was another remote, knowing that there wasn't. So we put all our hands out where they were in full view. "Turn to Channel 5," Brian said and the TV switched over to Channel 5. "Turn to channel 13." The TV does as it is asked. This was some experience. I have had lots of different experiences over the years but this was one whereby we were all there sharing the experience together.

I felt the energy shift in the room. I could feel Spirit energy right at the bottom of the bed. Brian decided to ask some different questions. He said to Tammy and me "It's my dad. It's Paddy." Tammy and I felt the same. Brian asked "Is this you, dad? If so, turn the TV off." Nothing happening for a few seconds then the TV switched off! Well the three of us nearly fell out of the bed! *Granddad it's you! Thanks so much for coming today.*

We were all excited. Brian asked "Is this really you, dad? If so, turn the TV on and switch to channel 6." There was a pause again and then the TV switched onto channel 1, then went onto 2, 3, 4, 5, 6 and stopped. "It's you dad! Thanks so much for coming and letting us all know you are around us." I could see Tammy and Brian well up a little, as did I. *We love you so much and miss you so much.* We sat there for the next few minutes without speaking a word.

I called my Spirit Guide, Danny. *Can you hear me, Danny?* I heard the word, 'yes.' *Can you tell my granddad I love him?* I heard, 'you could tell him' in reply. *What, he can hear me?* I then said *I love you granddad. We love you.* I heard softly in my mind. *I know. I am with you all the time.* I was so happy. Brian then said "I have one more question. Is it a good move for us to go back to Ireland?" If so, go back to channel 3." Without hesitation the TV went straight to channel 3. That was the confirmation Brian needed. It helped put away a lot of doubt. The TV switched off. I heard Danny say 'it's our time to go.' The room heated up again and they were gone.

We all had some excitement that day. The happiness I felt for my uncle Brian that day was unreal. I was so happy granddad came and gave him his sign that it was okay to move to Ireland and things would work out, and his confirmation that he was always near.

I was going to visit Sue-Ellen, she worked in a hair salon and she was going to give me a haircut and we were going to spend the day hanging out. I hadn't much time left in the states and I wanted to spend as much time with her before I left as we had such a great connection. I also wanted to see Paula before I left for Ireland, so I asked Sue-Ellen if she would like to come to the house the night Paula was calling to Brian and Tammy's. We were going to have a mini circle between us.

I was starting to think I didn't want to go back to Ireland so I confided with Sue-Ellen about this. She suggested I stay on and I could stay with her, I was really thinking about it—I felt so torn. It was okay having the support of Brian and Tammy, but if they went would I survive? Sue-Ellen was so generous and in some sense she was saying 'I will look after you.' But that old Irish pride just wouldn't let her do that. I needed to be a man.

I spoke to her about not being able to drive and it was a lot harder to get work outside of the city. She understood, but probably wasn't thinking things through fully. It simply wouldn't be realistic to stay.

At this time Sue-Ellen was going through a lot of stuff herself and was only getting her life back on track. So we agreed I would go home, look for work and stay for good. This was the plan. I also said I would love to go to see the Medium for a reading. She wanted to go also. I asked her to contact him and we would both go to see him together. Sue-Ellen called him and got his answering machine and left a message. She said she knew this other place that you could get a reading.

I waited at the salon until Sue-Ellen finished her shift. We got in the car and took a spin to this shop where the other reader was, they weren't working that day. The shop was really nice and there were lots of nice crystals and books. I went outside and waited for Sue-Ellen who was browsing in the shop. When she came out of the crystal shop she had bought a little gift. It was a bookmark which said faith and had a symbol on it. "I got this for you to represent your faith. When you read it you will see how strong your faith is." I was delighted. I thanked her for this perfect gift. Sue-Ellen informed me that the reader wouldn't be available for a couple of days. I was really looking for a reading before I came back to Ireland.

I was looking at my new bookmark and the symbol for faith. I really loved it. I decided to get a tattoo of the faith symbol done so every time I look at it would remind me Sue-Ellen, how strong I am and my faith.

I decided my wrist was the best place to get this special tattoo as I would be able to see it every day.

Everything comes to you for a reason, everything has its time and place, everything is happening perfectly.

Sue-Ellen dropped me home that evening. I looked into her I eyes and I knew that there was something really special about meeting her.

I went to bed that night. I had this symbol of faith and I was going to go get this tattoo, it felt so right. As I lay in bed I asked my usual questions to God about my life. *Where was I going and what I will I do?* I was asking my Angel what the true meaning of HOPE was. Why have you brought this to me? I kept saying HOPE over and over again. I must have drifted off at some stage. I woke at 3:33 am hearing these words ...

"It's Time to Wake Up—Your Answer Has Come!"

I was awakened out of my sleep and tried to bring my eyes into focus whilst turning my bedside lamp on. I heard her voice as soft as the first time "Can you hear me dear one? Your answer has come. It's time for me to tell you the meaning of 'HOPE'. Before I tell you, we have to say we are proud that you have come a long way since you looked for me at the garage and you did not find me, you never lost faith. I did warn you that you would doubt and you will still have times of doubt from now but your faith is what will save you. The answers you seek will come as I have told you before and it will be in divine timing. You are now starting to understand our energy and light again. You are working with your Spirit Guides now."

"Where are you? Why can't I see you?"

"Turn your lamp off and close your eyes," she gently instructed.

I felt the room get really warm. The energy in the room completed changed.

"Open your eyes slowly," she guided.

I began to open my eyes—all I can see is light so clear and bright. I asked, "Why am I seeing you this way?"

"Because this is what we really are! We only appear to each person as they can handle us or in the way they have been told about us or have really imagined us in their mind. When the time is right we will appear to them as you see me now. I come from the light of God. I can take many shapes and forms. I am showing you so you will recognise me and other Angels from now on."

"I have seen this light before," I say.

"Yes dear one, you have, but so have others."

She had a golden white light but there were many other colours simmering through her. The colour that was mostly around her silhouette was a white light which surrounded her.

"The white light you see is what some people describe as our wings."

"Will I see you or the other Angels in any other form?" I asked.

"Yes, I told you we will appear in many shapes and forms. You can see me tonight in my purest essence."

"Why have I been chosen for this? Why me? What can I do?"
I wondered.

"You have not been chosen. You have been the one to choose. You used your free will and your soul's agreement to live this life. You will not have every answer now as you will have to grow. As you do, your light will grow so others may see you."

"I feel things around people and my hands get tingly and hot,"
I replied.

"This is the energy from the heart of Mother and Father God and the universe. This energy you feel is within every single soul. You have the ability to use and connect to it. Dear one you choose this journey to help others. It's your wisdom from other life-times up to this you will share, be a beacon, not only to the light, but also to the darkness, help people to see their light. Sometimes it will be the darkness that you see mostly but remember we surround you in love from the great divine. It will be people's shadows you will see and on a soul level they will understand but in the physical they will try to hide their pain or disillusions. They may even try to hurt you. We are watching over you and protecting you. Don't fear, just be love and light. Remember the great teachers that have come before you. They will help you to bring their teaching to this world. The time will come when all will fall into place but up until then you will feel like you are being left behind. But the time will be perfect for you and this is when you will bring the message of HOPE and the Angels of HOPE to this world."

"What? The Angels of HOPE?"

"Yes, these Angels are Ascended beings and Masters of love and light, they will come forth bringing the true message of HOPE for each and every single soul on this earth. God's message is simply love and peace to all."

"So I am bringing the message?"

"Yes, HOPE and the Angels of HOPE. Our meaning for HOPE is ...

H = Help
O = Other
P = People
E = Evolve

When you bring HOPE to another soul you help that soul to see their light. Too many souls are helping themselves and not for the good of man, this needs to change so that humanity can change. So help other people means you help other people recognise their journey and tell them it is a journey of meaning. Help them to see the light that is within. It is very important to recognise the soul that is far worse off than you are, this will teach you compassion and take away the emptiness that is within. Don't cross the street to pass them by if someone should ask you for help. Help them. Give to them from your heart and not the mind—this is love. Don't give to receive. When you come from a place of love, you have already received. These are all simple principles that you must live by if you want to fulfil your life and destiny. You must all stand united hand in hand in peace and love and there shall not be one mouth that should go unfed. The time of war should come to an end. So you may all evolve not just a select few—it is not the will of God to leave one soul in the darkness. As I have explained before, we come from a place on high that most humans have yet to understand, but consciousness is changing to become aware.

"Help Other People Evolve—call upon the Angels of HOPE. This is your planet and it is this planet that needs to change the most. When I tell you these things tonight you will not share this for many years until the timing is right and your planet's vibration is being raised. This is the time when you will most need HOPE."

"I am only one person—how can I do this?" I asked her.

She replied "You will write books that we will channel to you, it's very important that you also keep a diary because they will be part of your books. The books will help you to bring our message of HOPE. You will also bring messages of guidance and healing to people from Angels and Spirit realms to Help Other People Evolve—HOPE. We will help you to write about your journey and how we have helped you to awaken so that others may see we are also helping them.

   It's important that you teach about learning to live a life that is full of gratitude, as this will bring many blessing to those who live by this. You will work with your healing gifts and we will bring you the knowledge you need to know about energy so you may show others. We will send People to you for healing and guidance and one day you will stand in front of people telling your story and talking about us."

"Really? But I can't write. I am left handed and I struggled for most of my life with this. I don't think I can do this, me be a writer. I failed English in school because I couldn't write well, I have always felt judged. I am not sure I can write a book."

I couldn't see this at the time. Everything was all so new and this just sounded like a mammoth task. I had started to write in a diary and this was a challenge! Little did I know that these diaries would one day serve such a purpose for me. She reassured me "Robert I know your journey in this life. I have been with you at every moment, don't be afraid to write, this will become much easier as we help you. The reason you struggled so much in school was because you had to

choose to keep your right side of the brain more open and anything
that defined logic would have suppressed you even more. So the battle
through education was all part of your awakening. I will help you
to understand all your lost memories so we will go back into your
childhood and work our way from there, so that will become part of the
second part of your story. You have an intelligence that has not come
from books. It comes from the very essence of your soul and it's your
journey now to awaken and share to the many others who are like you.
You will help people to wake up. So it's time to stop beating yourself
up. There is great healing to come your way and then through the help
of the Angels you will Help Other People Evolve".

"So I will remember things from my childhood? There are parts I feel
I need to know about because I feel this is where a lot of my blocks
and karma come from." "Yes. We will help you remember all that you
need from your childhood right up to the present so you may help
others. The answers will not come tonight so be patient is what I am
reminding you of. Trust in us and your coin will guide you along the
journey. There will be many people who will hold your coin and this
will also bring them great healing, hope and faith. So the answer is,
you are just one seed but from this many others will grow. If you build
they will come. Have faith, God has a divine plan for you and one day
you will look back and this won't seem as unreal as it does now. What
you will teach will be that the only one true answer in this world will
be one of love and peace. Don't be afraid to speak from your heart as
we will guide you with every single word that you need."

Love and peace?

She hears my thoughts, "Yes that is it.

You just answered my thoughts!

"Yes. We can connect to your thoughts. I am like your filter for
protection and guidance, as the gatekeepers watching over the souls
of this earth. One day each and every soul will remember this. Our
message for you and each and every other soul is to always go back to
your creation, the great I AM Presence: God. This will always be the

only answer for it is God's love that you know best. It is God's will for you all to remember that. Your coin will be a symbol of HOPE—you will be the beacon of light to which it will come. I am with you at every moment, just call me when you are most in need and I will come. You are now working with your Spirit family and Angels. It will take time to learn how to communicate and understand fully so don't lose patience!"

I thanked her again and with that she was gone.

I fell back to sleep straight away. I slept like a baby. When I awoke the next morning my first thoughts were to the meaning of HOPE—Help Other People Evolve. The answer was one of service and how best to serve others.

I had the poem **Footprints in the Sand** ringing through my mind, which I had seen every single day as a child and as a young adult. It hung on the wall in my grandmother's bathroom so you couldn't help read it every time as you went in! I never fully understood that, but now I do know the true meaning.

(Song—*Pure Imagination* Anthony Newley/Leslie Bruciuse—from the movie Willy Wonka & the Chocolate Factory)

God is everything God is real, so real. I have received more than one validation in my life. God has answered my prayers, helping me to let go of any old patterns and thoughts that I once struggled with. The answer I received was God is, and will always be talked about in books, and there will be many rules that will be made in the name of God but really the truth is within us all. There are no rules to what God is, it is no one thing and it is everything. There are no limits or no description on this earth that can describe the source of God and creation. All creation is energy, everything in creation is energy. Remember that you have a straight connection and when you know this you have your own know, not someone else's interpretation. It's beyond thought therefore we will call it all that is ever was and ever will be. If you continually search for a messiah outside of yourself, you may miss God because God is your feelings, your experience, everything that you are. God isn't what you believe, it's what you are and what you do. Knowing is your own experience and belief is just a system someone else preaches. Do not tell me but show me. The limitations of language, time and space may hinder my explanation but my soul knows God and your soul knows God. There is no hierarchy of communication between your soul and God. It just is.

Mother and Father God were speaking to me showing that the vastness of their love and how expansive it is. The 'I Am' presence that is within us all, connecting us to each and every single thought and emotion. I was shown that there is a God outside of the books we have all been taught from. The love of God to and for us, is untouchable.

I was beginning to learn to live my life outside of the dogma of others. This was my starting journey—to learn to read between the lines and not let others try to control my path with misguided information. God is and always has been unconditional love, shining forth to their children of this earth. God has not only brought me validations, sent to me my guardian Angel, but this is for you and coming from the sceptic to a place where I can begin to find harmony. This was something God's love has always been trying to show me, but it has been the will of people that has caused separation because they come from fear based Ego. When I start to look back it has always been about control but even through this God's love has never left me nor will it leave you.

19

We Are All One!

Brian was telling me about all the bits and pieces they had to do before moving back to Ireland. They were planning on flying into Ireland and then going back to America to finalise things before moving back. I thought I might come back to America with them and stay with Sue-Ellen. I decided not to tell Brian about my Angel coming to me that night as I didn't feel it was the right time for me to talk about it. I was keeping lots of things very closely to my heart. I was still learning and growing through my own pain and understanding.

I wanted to get some stuff at Wal-Mart so Tammy took me over. I was looking for some things to bring home. I didn't pick up too much as money was tight. When we got back Brian said Sue-Ellen had called. I phoned her straight away, "What's up?" I ask.

"You'll never guess what? I got us that appointment for the Medium?"

"No way! You're joking!"

"No, I am not!"

I was really excited. I couldn't wait to see him. It seemed that everything was falling into place.

Circle

Paula and Sue-Ellen arrived at Brian and Tammy's for our circle. I told Paula about all that had been happening lately with the Medium. She said that I would be doing that work soon! I thanked her again for the healing as I felt it helped me to open up so much. The conversation was great, so open—we all got on so well. I was telling them that Sue-Ellen got an appointment to see the Medium and I couldn't wait. Paula then started talking about healing and meditation. I really enjoyed listening to her knowledge and wisdom. She brought us through a lovely guided meditation calling in our Spirit Guides and asking for their names.

I already knew mine was called Danny. Sue-Ellen and I were sitting on the chair together, we could all feel the room get cold. We looked at each other as the energy started to move around us. The room was full of Spirit energy. I could feel Danny but I could feel others too. My Granddad was there and there was a mixture of Angels and Spirit. This was my training ground helping me to understand different experiences. This was a time when I started to build on my vocabulary—my language with the Angels and Spirits. We all just really enjoyed the moment and it was so much fun. Everyone was feeling this, not just a select one or two, proving that it was there for all of us. God does not have one favourite but a love for each and every one of us. What this also showed us was that on our own we are strong but united we are stronger—we can hold more energy. It was the universe saying there was no special recipe—if you show up they would turn up!

The night was coming to end. Paula offered to teach Brian and I Reiki. She really felt it would help us on our path. Paula was so kind and wanted to share everything coming from the heart.

Faith

I wanted to get the tattoo so I had asked Brian to drive me as it meant so much to me. I wanted to get it as a memory of my Spiritual connection to Sue-Ellen. We arrived at the tattoo parlour to be greeted by a tall long-haired guy covered in tattoos. He looked at me and said "You looking for a tattoo?"

I nod "Yes."

"What do you want?"

I showed him the bookmark with the faith symbol. He started laughing at me, "I am not doing that! It's way too small. I only do big tattoos. He looked to his assistant "Would you do that?" I looked at her and smiled. She laughed "Yes, if he really wants it."

"I have won lots of competitions and been in loads of magazines. I couldn't say that this is my work," he said.

"This really means a lot to me," I said.

"So where do you want this tiny tattoo?" he asked.

"On my wrist—it means faith," I said.

"Faith in what?" he asked.

"In God," I said proudly. This was the first time I had ever said anything about God to a complete stranger. I wasn't afraid of his judgements.

He looked at the picture and drew it free-hand. It took him about five minutes! I couldn't wait to show Sue-Ellen. I went to see her later that day at the saloon. When I got there she was a little pissed off as she really wanted to go with me. I didn't realise she wanted to get the same tattoo. I tried to talk her out of it as I thought that it wouldn't be a good idea for her work. But she really wanted it done so she finished up work early and we drove to the tattoo parlour. As luck would have it, it was closed. The tattoo 'faith' wasn't meant for her that day.

I had phoned home a couple of times. We decided that I would surprise everyone for my sisters 21st birthday. I was going to get the chance to see all of my friends and family. I was trying to really think what they would be like when they saw me. I wasn't drinking or smoking anymore.

I would now spend my time writing in a journal, meditating and reading books. My family were in for a shock! They will wonder where the party animal had gone! In America I was surrounded by so many like-minded people. I knew going home that all my friends and family were not into Angels. Thinking about myself and developing my gift and learning was a little daunting. *What will my life be like back in Ireland? I won't stay for long—I'll go home for a few weeks and then book a flight back—I'll take my chances back in America.*

Appointment with the Medium

It was an early morning appointment. Sue-Ellen was running a little late as the roads were bad. I was ready and watching the clock. I saw Sue-Ellen's car pulling in so I made my way out to the car. I was excited and so was Sue-Ellen. I wondered if he would say I was to stay in America with her. I also wondered if he was going to mention Sue-Ellen as we had developed feelings for each other.

We were running late for the first appointment so we called but got no answer. I asked the Angels to help us get there in time and to give us green lights. We arrived about 20 minute's late. I knocked on the door but there was no answer. I knocked on a couple of windows and put my hands up to the glass but there didn't seem to be any sign of anyone there. I was starting to think that we weren't going to see this guy. So I was back in the car "What will we do?" I asked. Sue-Ellen suggested we wait a few more minutes. I felt the butterflies in my tummy and my hands started to get a little sweaty. I asked my Guide Danny what was happening, but I got no answer. All of a sudden the Medium came to the door and waved us up. Sue-Ellen and I were debating who would go first—each of us wanted the other one to go first! We couldn't decide.

The Medium greeted us at the door and told us he only had one appointment as something urgent had come up for him. I told Sue-Ellen to take the appointment as she booked them. Sue-Ellen insisted I take the appointment as I was going home and she could go another time. The Medium then suggested we both get the reading together.

So off we went into his reading room—it was off the main space where he held the circle. I loved his energy. He was a straight talker, no bullshit. He said it the way it was. I think we were both a little nervous sharing the reading in case some things came out that we didn't want to hear!

Straight away he picked up on Spirit. He was really quick. He started giving messages—they were for Sue-Ellen. It was some family members in the Spirit world. He gave dates and initials. Sue-Ellen started to get emotional. I could feel her emotion, she had so much hurt and pain. He then spoke about the break-down of her marriage and the hurt she had been through. He was getting everything right.

He then moved over to me. He said "I have a young man here for you. He is giving me the letter to his name, P. He is also showing me a sudden impact, a crash, but not in a car, it was a bike." This was my friend who crashed his bike in 2001. "He's letting you know he's okay and happy you have chosen a different path in life. He is also speaking about a guy called Lee." This was his other mate. "He wants him to know he is okay." Lee was the last person to see him before he crossed over. I think he was blaming himself. "Tell Lee not to blame himself anymore. He wants to say he loves him." The Medium is giving lots of other information to us. Then my grandfather came into the room. I was feeling all the energies as they came into the room and so was Sue-Ellen. The Medium said, "This man is back again. He has been with me a few times. He always pushes his way up front to talk." I laughed. "He also has another man with him. You have spoken with your Spirit Guide." "Yes," I replied. "He has brought another Guide with him today. I am being told you are working with them both." All of a sudden I hear the name Tommy ringing in my ear. "His name is Tommy. Your grandfather keeps saying the name Joey." I must have got some psychic amnesia because not for the life of me could I think of a person called Joey. *My mom's name begins with J—Jacinta, my little brothers name j—Jason, my grandfather had a budgie called Joey—is this what he means?* The Medium insists "Joey, do know this name?" I looked at Sue-Ellen—*did she know someone by the name of Joey?* "Whoever this is tell him he needs to grow up. He is in the wrong company," he warned. "I'm sorry you're wrong, there is no Joey in my family." I had complete amnesia.

The reading continued ....

"You are going home to Ireland. You won't be back to America for many years." I was planning on coming back in a month or two maximum. "If you're not back in America in a month you won't be back for a long time."

"Will I do the same work as you?" I asked.

"Yes, you are connecting with other worlds. I can see you doing this work. You are a great healer."

Sue-Ellen and I were both happy with our readings. We got into the car "Who the hell is Joey?" We both were racking our brains to think who this person was when about half a mile away my mind just opened up and I said "Shit, Joey is my older brother!"

As we made our way back to Brian and Tammy's all I could think about was doing Mediumship as my work. I wasn't sure how it would happen, but I just knew it would. Sue-Ellen and I didn't really talk about him saying I may not come back to America.

When Sue-Ellen dropped me off she said she had a little gift for me. "I will give it to you the next time I'm over."

"What is it?"

"It's a surprise. I will see you later, okay?"

"Thanks for today. I am so grateful."

I thanked Spirit for today and for my new Spirit Guide Tommy. I was really looking forward to connecting with him.

My Surprise

Sue-Ellen called around to pick me up and we went out for some food. We were chatting about the future and our future. "I have your gift with me tonight. I got you a little something. You can open one, but I don't want you to open the other until you are on the plane home." It was wrapped like it was a book. I unwrapped the other present—it was a little pouch that said HOPE on the outside of it. I pulled the strings apart and emptied the contents onto my hand. It was two beautiful silver Angels, one bigger than the other. The biggest one was the Angel of Hope and the other was the Angel of Love. This was the most amazing gift ever!

I felt like crying because of the thought that she had put into them. They were perfect for the journey I was about to embark on in my life. I kissed her and thanked her so much. My words were not able to express how much this really meant to me. This was so thoughtful. I had my coin in a cloth. I took it out and I put the three of them together.

From that day until the present day they have remained together and have never been separate from each other for one moment. They have never been separate from me, they have been in my pocket and they have sat by my bed every single night over these years, guiding me.

We spent the rest of the evening together talking about so many things, thanking the universe for putting us together for the shortest time ever—only 6 weeks! She made me promise not to open the other gift until my plane took off. I promised. We spent the rest of that night holding each other.

It was the day before I flew home and Brian, Tammy and I were checking things off our lists. I was feeling a little nervous about getting out of the country safely. The airline emailed Tammy looking for the number of my holiday visa. It was the number of the waiver visa you fill in when you come into the country. They take it back off you when you leave. I ripped the piece of paper with the number on it out of my passport based on the advice from a friend who told me if I got stopped to say I lost it and then they wouldn't know how long I was there for. Brian told me not to worry that lots of people would do that. I think he was only saying this to me to make me feel better! I called on her my Guardian Angel *please help me here. I give you my permission.* I was all packed up and ready to go. I had decided to try and ring Kim one last time to say goodbye and thank you.

I was just about to phone Kim. I asked my Guides and Angels, *please help me out here.* I picked up the phone and made the call. It was ringing and ringing. I was about to hang up when Kim finally answered. "Hello, it's me Robbie." I knew by her voice that she didn't want to speak. "You may not want to speak to me but I have to tell you that I am sorry Kim for hurting you. I am leaving tomorrow to go back home to Ireland."

"I knew this would happen Robbie," she said.

There was a silence. "I never planned for it to work out this way, it just happened." I think she knew at this point that it wasn't my plan to hurt her. It wasn't something I had set out to do. I felt she was still hurting so our conversation was short. I felt so sad that she was hurting but I had to let go of the pain and when I did it felt like a massive weight had been lifted off my shoulders.

To always know that everything is always happening for a reason and sometimes in life when we are in middle of it, is when we can't see it. It doesn't mean that it's not all still happening perfectly. We and we alone are the only person driving our ship, no one else will see through your eyes just like no one else will see the last thing before you sleep and the first thing when you awake. We have to make choices in this life. Sometimes that can be hurtful or may cause pain and others may seem effortless but it's always happening. Taking responsibility is our biggest lesson but it will not be our only one.

I spent the day before I was due to leave visiting Tammy's family and some friends I had made to say my farewells. As a wise man one once told me, you only ever say goodbye to a person if you'll see them again, if for any reason you think you may never see that person again, it is always better to say 'I will see you later.'

I was sad at the thought of leaving Sue-Ellen. For such a short time that we knew each other, we had shared so much. Through my sadness I was so grateful for my journey in America—what a roller coaster ride it was leaving Ireland lost, going through all my experiences to have found myself again! I had found HOPE. My faith was now sealed. My belief was rock solid. Through every single moment I have been blessed and looked after. My new job would be working for the universe. The soul had found the soul thus giving the soul a purpose.

27-1-2003

It Was My Time to Leave

It was time to go. I asked Sue-Ellen to mind some stuff for me until I came back. I double checked everything to make sure I had my passport, my coin and Angel gifts in my pocket. Sue-Ellen was so quiet. I knew when I looked at her she wanted to cry. I had a lump in my own throat but I felt I had to be strong. Everyone was ready so we started packing up the car. I was thinking about the airport a little and asking my Spirit Guides to mind me.

Sue-Ellen was crying and I was crying too. I gave her a hug and I whispered into her ear "I'll meet you there." Somewhere on a soul level our time was up. I hugged her tightly "I will see you later." I closed the car door and it started to pull off. Sue-Ellen was standing in the middle of the drive on her own crying. I was looking back and as we got further away she was getting smaller and smaller until I couldn't see her anymore. I spent most of the drive just staring into space daydreaming—contemplating my whole experience.

The Airport

As we approached the airport I was feeling nervous and anxious in case I got caught. I could feel the presence of my Guides around me. We made our way over to the Aer Lingus check in desk. Tammy could see I was really anxious. My knees where knocking and let me tell you it was very visible. My hands were even rattling! Tammy got me to hold one of one the kid's hands as she thought it would relax me and it did. We were at the check-in desk. I had my passport in my hand, standing in line and it was my turn next. A young Irish–American guy was working on the desk. I handed him my passport and he asked me "Were you over for long? "Just a couple of months" I replied. He looked at my passport and asked "Where is your holiday visa waiver?" Now this is all post 911 so things are a lot tighter security wise. I explained that I lost my holiday visa waiver. He gave me a funny look. He looked at the date with the stamp that I arrived in 2001. I asked my Angel, *please help me!* I saw lots of light around him—I knew my Angels were helping. He looked at my passport again. "There is one of the pages signed, did you know that?" he asked. "Yes, a famous singer signed his autograph on my password on a night out," I replied.

    Let me rewind the clock just a tick. Whilst I was living in Manhattan I went to a bar one day with one of my buddies. There was an Open Mike session on. A friend of mine worked behind the bar, it was called the Red Loin in the village in Manhattan. We were drinking away when we noticed a famous singer by the name of Shawn Mullen appeared. He sang that song called *Rock a Bye*. I was a little star struck so I bought him a pint and we ended up having a few beers with him! Before he left I asked him to give me his autograph but the only thing I had was my passport. He very hesitantly signed it. Oops, maybe that wasn't such a good idea after all!

So I was standing at the airport check-in waiting for the SWAT team to jump me! Slightly paranoid! I saw this really bright ocean blue colour behind him—it is the Archangel Michael. He dropped something on the floor and when he got back up he stamped my passport and said "Okay, enjoy your flight." *Thank you, thank you, thank you!*

(Song—*Now we are free* Lisa Gerrard—Gladiator movie)

We boarded the plane. I was sitting in my seat waiting for the door to close; as we were still on American soil I still didn't feel 100% free. It's amazing how the mind can be so irrational when filled with fear. It's funny, I wasn't a criminal, granted I over stayed my welcome but it was all part of my path, my divine plan and my soul's agreement. The captain spoke over the PA system saying we were ready to taxi to the runway. The Stewarts locked the door and I felt a massive sense of relief. The engines fired up and we were off ... the front wheels left the ground and I was no longer on American soil. I was about to begin a whole new part of my journey.

I remembered that I still had Sue-Ellen's gift to open. I looked inside the bag and opened it thinking it was a book, but it wasn't, it was a diary, a beautiful hard-backed writing book. I opened it and I come to the first page and there was a written message ...

01-23-2003

Dear Robbie,

Some people only worry about getting the best out of life. Few
people like you, special people like you, know that it's more important
to give life your best.

You're dreaming new dreams, learning new things and accepting new
challenges. Some people are afraid of opening new doors and taking
risks, but you are not like that. You're strong, your faith is powerful and
will guide you to new levels, higher levels.

Moment by moment, day by day you are becoming the person you
want to be. You are someone I admire and someone I am proud to
know.

Especially, you're someone that I believe in and someone who has
taught me a lot about love, faith and how to cherish life.

Thank you for all that you have given me.

I'll meet you there.

Love,
Sue-Ellen xx

To be continued ....

*I would like to share this beautiful poem that was given to me from a
client who then became a very dear friend. The poem was channelled
to Sandra Poland Barry by her Angels about my journey and coin. I
absolutely love this poem and I am so grateful for the Angels bringing
me such a kind friend. Heartfelt gratitude to you, Sandra. Thank you.*